UNIT

OCR | A2 | F297

Business Studies

Strategic Management

Andy Mottershead, Alex Grant and
Judith Kelt

Philip Allan Updates, an imprint of Hodder Education, an Hachette UK company, Market Place, Deddington, Oxfordshire OX15 0SE

Orders

Bookpoint Ltd, 130 Milton Park, Abingdon, Oxfordshire OX14 4SB
tel: 01235 827827
fax: 01235 400401
e-mail: education@bookpoint.co.uk
Lines are open 9.00 a.m.–5.00 p.m., Monday to Saturday, with a 24-hour message answering service. You can also order through the Philip Allan Updates website: www.philipallan.co.uk

© Andy Mottershead, Alex Grant and Judith Kelt

ISBN 978-1-4441-1563-5

First printed 2010
Impression number 5 4 3 2 1
Year 2014 2013 2012 2011 2010

This guide has been written specifically to support students preparing for the OCR A2 Business Studies Unit F297 examination. The content has been neither approved nor endorsed by OCR and remains the sole responsibility of the authors.

Typeset by MPS Limited, a Macmillan Company
Printed by MPG Books, Bodmin

Hachette UK's policy is to use papers that are natural, renewable and recyclable products and made from wood grown in sustainable forests. The logging and manufacturing processes are expected to conform to the environmental regulations of the country of origin.

P01772

101126

A2 Business Studies

Contents

Introduction

About this guide 5

Key elements 5

How to revise 10

■ ■ ■

Content Guidance

About this section 14

Objectives 15

Strategic planning 17

Stakeholder objectives and strategic management 20

Market analysis 22

Forecasting (time series analysis) 24

Decision trees 27

Measures of business performance (people) 31

The nature of economic activity 33

The economic cycle 35

The macroeconomic objectives of government 38

Economic policy and its effect on businesses 40

The exchange rate 43

The European Union 47

Businesses and the law 49

Political issues 52

Social change 54

Technological change 56

The environment 58

The management of change 61

Change within the business 63

Industrial relations and change 65

■ ■ ■

Questions & Answers

About this section 70

Case study: Learning for Life Ltd 71

■ ■ ■

Appendix

Detailed mark scheme 92

Introduction

About this guide

The aim of this guide is to help you to maximise your grade in the OCR examination: Strategic Management (F297). The information contained in the guide has been organised to mirror the textbook, *OCR Business Studies for A2* by Andy Mottershead, Alex Grant and Judith Kelt. This order reflects the order of the topics within the OCR specification. If you have not got a copy of the specification, it is worth downloading from the OCR website (www.ocr.org.uk), as you will then be able to tick off the topics as your revision progresses.

The guide is divided into clear sections to make your revision easier.

(1) Introduction. This explains the key elements that you need to understand if you are to gain a high grade. It will help you to realise what an examiner is looking for and how he or she will award you marks. It also outlines the strategies that you can adopt in order to revise successfully.

(2) Content Guidance. This section, which closely follows the OCR specification, outlines all the topics on which you may be tested in the examination.

(3) Questions and Answers. In this section there is a case study for you to attempt. The case study is very similar to what you can expect to see in your examination. There are exactly the same number and type of questions to enable you to become familiar with the format of the paper. Sample A-grade answers are provided to help you see what is required to reach this grade. Examiner's comments explain how each candidate answer is awarded marks, and highlight the exact point at which a particular level is awarded, so that you can quickly and easily adopt a similar strategy in your answers. The comments also indicate why some students' answers fail to achieve an A grade.

Key elements

Levels of response

One of the key routes to success is understanding levels of response. Answering a question using the appropriate level of response will mean that you are approaching the question in the right manner.

Understanding how examiners use 'trigger words' (see p. 7) will help you to identify which level of response is required.

Level of response	Definition
Level 1	**Knowledge** • Business knowledge or facts
Level 2	**Explanation or application** • An explanation or understanding of knowledge
Level 3	**Analysis** • Implications for the business • How the business is affected • The reaction of a business or stakeholder All should be in the context of the case.
Level 4	**Evaluation** • Making a justified judgement in the context of the case • Weighing the evidence/arguments long term and short term in the context of the case • Suggesting which issue raised is the most significant, the most likely to affect the business or the most serious factor to affect the business

Mastering what is required for each level of response should be a high priority. You will be able to practise this skill later in the book in the Questions and Answers section.

Ensuring that you are able to offer analysis and evaluation is essential if you are to achieve the top grades. Consider the example of Business A, which is about to invest in new technology by buying a new machine. The following paragraphs show how easy it is to gain a Level 3 (L3) mark.

Analysis

The owners of the business will be able to produce more items as the new machine is much more efficient. Therefore with more goods being produced, the business will be able to increase its revenue from the extra sales. This additional revenue will help the business to make more profit (L3) and therefore it will be able to offer a higher dividend to its shareholders (L3).

Being able to produce more goods with the new machine may, however, lead to a fall in the number of employees who are needed. The employees may therefore either lose their jobs or be fearful of losing their jobs, which may affect their productivity (L3).

With the new machine and the subsequent increase in output, the suppliers to the business will have the opportunity to sell more of their components and therefore increase their sales revenue. It may mean the suppliers will need to take on more employees (L3), which will benefit the government, as it will have to pay out less in job seeker's allowance (L3).

Clearly stating the likely implications for the business or stakeholders, or how the business may react, in the context of the case is a common and effective way in which to gain Level 3 marks.

Similarly, evaluative statements require you to make a justified judgement. The judgement can be related to the most likely effect, or the factor that will have the most beneficial or detrimental effect upon the business. The following paragraph shows you how to achieve Level 4 (L4) by using evaluation.

Evaluation

The stakeholder which will benefit the most is likely to be the shareholder. As a result of the increased output from the new machine, it is very likely that the increased sales will mean additional profits that could be distributed in the form of dividends to the shareholders. This is more certain than the possibility of redundancies as a result of the machine. It is not certain if the machine is used instead of employees. With the increased output the firm may actually require additional employees and not fewer (L4).

The candidate has made a judgement which suggests that one group of stakeholders will benefit more than another and has justified this view in the context of the case.

It is not enough just to begin your answer 'In evaluation' — you have to make an actual judgement that has been justified in context. There may be clues within the case as to the long-term objectives of the business. In that case some of the evaluative comments can concentrate on the ability of the technology to help achieve the long-term aims.

Trigger words

Trigger words for the questions and the appropriate levels of response required are listed in the table below. Levels of response are also referred to as assessment objectives (AOs).

Trigger words

Trigger words	Level of response	Assessment objectives
State, list	Level 1	AO1
Explain, outline, describe	Level 2	AO2
Analyse	Level 3	AO3
Evaluate, assess, to what extent, discuss, recommend	Level 4	AO4

It is important to realise that for A2, the emphasis is on your ability to offer appropriate analysis and evaluation in the context of the case. It is also important to note that the weighting of the mark allocation changes significantly for A2 when compared to AS (see the table below).

Weightings for assessment objectives (levels of response): A2 marks

Strategic Management	AO1 (L1)	AO2 (L2)	AO3 (L3)	AO4 (L4)	Total
Q1a	3	5	5		13
Q1b	3	4	4	7	18
Q2	3	4	4	7	18
Q3	3	4	4	7	18
Q4	4	6	6	7	23
Totals	16	23	23	28	90
					60% of A2
Introduction to Business AS	14%	10%	10%	6%	40% of AS

Examination format for F297 Strategic Management

It is important that you are aware of the examination format. Your teacher will no doubt have made this clear to you at an early stage in the course.
- length of examination: 2 hours
- the total marks for this paper represent 60% of the total A2 marks.

This is a pre-issued case study paper, where the stimulus material is approximately four to five sides of A4 in length. The questions are answered in an answer booklet, where each question is followed by a space in which you write your answer.

There are four questions, which can come from any section of the specification. The questions will require you to evaluate, and therefore this skill will be essential.

The first question is now subdivided into two parts, and consequently you will need to take care over how much time and how much to write for parts (l) (a) and (b).

Unit F297 contains a compulsory numerical question. This will usually be a question on:
- decision trees
- critical path analysis (network analysis)
- time series analysis
- ratios

It is hoped that studying the pre-issued case study will give you some indication of which is to be examined.

Tackling the case study

It is essential that you are able to use the context of the case. In order to do this, it is worthwhile adopting the 'first read' and 'second read' approach.

First read

Read the case quickly to ascertain:

- the type of business (its legal status — Ltd, plc sole trader) and its age or size
- the product or service
- the consumers
- the objectives of the business

These four factors will provide you with a framework in which to answer the questions.

Second read

Read the questions and then read the case again. This is a more thorough read when you can start looking for information within the case to answer the questions posed.

For Unit F297, the several pages of case material provide a wealth of context for you to use. For Level 3 and Level 4 answers, you are expected to use the context in order to gain the marks.

It is important to remember that there will be some data (numerical information) within the case. It is essential that you actually use it, even though it contains numbers — something that puts some students off. Actually, the information within the numbers is often crucial and may tell you something about the state of the business. There is a wealth of information within any financial accounts that are offered to you. Give these serious attention, as you will be able to assess the state of the business by calculating several ratios that can then be used to offer justification for your views.

Similarly, it is vital that you state any formulae you use and ensure that your working is clearly laid out in order to help examiners. There are marks to be gained for following this advice.

It may be helpful on the second read to note, in the margin of the question paper, lines that will be useful for answering a particular question. This will then enable you to quickly decide which of these points represent the key factors and which are not as important in answering a particular question.

The Principal Examiner's report, issued after each examination session, regularly suggests that the ability to use business terminology, theories and concepts accurately matters, and therefore it is important for you to take care when presenting your views within an answer.

Of more importance is an ability to read the question set. As this module is pre-issued, there is a danger of guessing what the questions will be and being caught out on the day when the wording changes the emphasis of the question. It is dangerous to assume that you know what will be asked.

Answering the questions: ABC

A Remember: although there is new material to be learnt for this module, it is also a 'synoptic' paper and therefore it is assumed you will have remembered material from your AS modules.

B When answering questions in this module, try using the mnemonic LOSER:
- LOng-term objectives
- Stakeholders
- External environment
- Resources

This is a very useful way to remember that the answers to the questions set should be addressed in such a manner as to cover these important issues. The word 'strategy' relates to an overview. Try to consider how the business within the case will be affected by events in terms of its objectives.
- Will events make these objectives easier or harder to achieve?
- How will the stakeholders of the business be affected?
- Will some of the stakeholders be affected more than others?
- How will external factors affect the business?
- Which of the external factors are the most significant?
- Does the business have sufficient resources to achieve what it wants to achieve?

C Try to offer a balanced answer. This means considering the positive and negative factors for the business. Once this has been attempted, it will be easier to offer a justified judgement in the context of the case.

Then check: did you...?
- answer the actual question (and not the one you were hoping would be asked)?
- note the trigger word?
- apply the right level in your answer — in context?
- note the mark allocation to ensure you used your time wisely?
- use the case to offer evidence for your views?
- offer comments on how the business would be affected or how it would react, in order to gain Level 3 marks?
- make a justified judgement for Level 4 answers?
- answer *all* the questions?

If you have answered yes to all of the bullet points, you have definitely improved your chances of gaining a good grade!

How to revise

You have already made a good start by looking at this guide! Time spent reading each section with care will be time well spent.
- There is no correct way to revise. Use whichever strategy bests suits you. If you prefer a particular learning style, use that style.
- Find out when your examinations are and plot them on a spreadsheet or calendar. This will help you organise your revision and prioritise which subjects are to be examined first.

- Ensure you use the 'Content Guidance' section of this guide as a checklist of all the topics you need to know.
- Remember that this is a synoptic paper and therefore you will need to revisit AS topics.
- If appropriate to your learning style, write out on index cards or in a small notebook the key points for each topic. Using cards or a small notebook ensures that you do not feel that there is so much to learn. Either format allows you to carry your notes around with you.   .
- For topics that you find hard to remember, it may be helpful to make a larger copy of the key words, formulae or diagrams, and stick this to your bedroom wall. A quick read-through of these before going to sleep can work wonders!
- Work on your revision in manageable periods of time to suit you. Good effective revision should be tackled in 20–30-minute sessions, rewarding yourself with a break, for example, once a set of cards have been prepared. However long your revision session is, reward yourself with the same time period for resting.
- You will need to extend this period of time when you start to practise the actual examination papers provided within this guide.
- Once you have finished a complete set of revision cards, you should practise examination questions to see if you can apply the information on the cards.
- Practise reading the question to note the trigger word and then just write a list of the knowledge (key concepts and terms) you would include in the answer.
- Practise the levels of response within your answers — think how the business in the case will be affected or how it might need to react (Level 3 — analysis). Try offering a justified judgement (Level 4 — evaluation).
- Ensure you practise within the time scale of the examination (2 hours). If you are a candidate who is entitled to extra time, build that extra time into your practice.
- Compare your answers with those provided within this guide and also check the 'Did you?' checklist above.

Content Guidance

The topics in this Content Guidance section appear in the same order as in the OCR specification. They also match the chapters in the *OCR Business Studies for A2* textbook by Andy Mottershead, Alex Grant and Judith Kelt, published by Hodder Education.

- Objectives
- Strategic planning
- Stakeholder objectives and strategic management
- Market analysis
- Forecasting (time series analysis)
- Decision trees
- Measures of business performance (people)
- The nature of economic activity
- The economic cycle
- The macroeconomic objectives of government
- Economic policy and its effect on businesses
- The exchange rate
- The European Union
- Businesses and the law
- Political issues
- Social change
- Technological change
- The environment
- The management of change
- Change within the business
- Industrial relations and change

Objectives

In discussing objectives, you will need to incorporate a discussion of all areas of the business and be able to show how the actions of one department affect the others. Objectives may be long term or short term. The communication of objectives to large numbers of people may be difficult for managers, but if this is done effectively, the end result is much more likely to be successful.

A mission statement

A mission statement:
- sets out the purpose of the business
- includes information about values
- may include the firm's policy on the environment and ethics
- makes all those involved in the business aware of its aims and objectives
- is not an end in itself — the business must ensure that the values in the mission statement impact on every action in its day-to-day business.

Aims and objectives

The aims of a business depend on a number of factors including:
- the age of the business
- the size of the business
- the market in which the business trades
- whether the business is in the private or public sector
- the wishes and priorities of the owner or the board of directors.

Strategic objectives

Any business will have one or more of the following strategic objectives:
- survival
- profitability
- growth
- market share.

The achievement of strategic or long-term objectives will require tactical or short-term objectives to be put in place (see F291 Module 1).

Survival
- In its early years, a business needs to establish itself in the market.
- Start-up costs are likely to be high. Loans may have been taken out from banks or friends and family. These will need to be repaid.
- Profitability is difficult to achieve in the early months and years. Cashflow may be the main problem faced by a business at this stage. This is the main reason for failure in new businesses.
- Setting realistic objectives is vitally important at this stage.

Profit

- The amount of profit the firm sets as an objective will depend very much on the wishes of those running the business.
- Some sole traders will make a balance between profit, working hours and quality of life their strategic objective.
- Larger businesses may find this objective dictated or constrained by the wishes of shareholders or the financial markets.

Growth and market share

- Once established, the business may wish to gain a competitive advantage.
- This is likely to involve growth into different areas of an existing market or into new markets.
- Ansoff's matrix lays out the possible strategies for growth available to a business.

Product growth

	Existing	New
Existing	Market penetration	Product development
New	Market development	Diversification

Market growth

Market penetration — existing product in existing market

Product development — new product in existing market

Market development — existing product in new market

Diversification — new product in new market

Figure 1 Ansoff's Matrix

Other strategic objectives

Part of a business's strategic objectives may involve satisfying other stakeholder objectives. These may include:

- shareholder returns (earnings per share)
- market leadership and status
- diversification into new markets to spread risk
- environmental or ethical concerns.

Stakeholder objectives

- Traditionally, businesses have wanted to achieve the maximum returns for their owners. That is not now the case. Managers now need to respond to a range of stakeholders.
- These include customers, employees, the bank and the community.
- Customers are increasingly interested in environmental and ethical concerns.
- A business that treats its employees well will usually be rewarded by motivation and loyalty.
- Paying suppliers quickly will often result in greater cooperation.

Stakeholder conflicts

- At times, the demands of one group of stakeholders may conflict with those of another.
- The need for profit for shareholders may conflict with demands for 'greener' production from customers. A business might be prepared to use more costly distribution channels if they result in a smaller carbon footprint.
- The requirement to treat employees well may result in higher costs for companies.

Risk and reward

- When setting objectives, businesses will need to balance the demands of risk and reward.
- For businesses in areas like pharmaceuticals and electronics, it may be necessary to take risks and to spend large amounts on research in order to achieve future profits and stay ahead of the competition.
- Some sectors and businesses, however, will be risk averse. This will limit their ability to make large profits and be competitive.

Analysis

There are many opportunities for analysis using objectives. It is possible to discuss the effect of choosing a particular objective on revenue or profitability or to analyse the effect on a variety of stakeholders. For example, if a business makes growth its main objective, this may mean that the shareholders need to accept lower dividends to enable the firm to invest in new equipment.

Evaluation

Choosing growth as an objective will have a variety of short- and long-term implications for the firm and its stakeholders. Dividends may be lower in the short term, but the long-term result should be improved profitability and better dividends. Discussion that weighs up these implications for the business and its stakeholders will gain evaluation marks.

Strategic planning

Planning for the future is an important aspect of any business, regardless of its size. Successful businesses plan for the future in all sorts of ways.

- Is it necessary to introduce new products?
- How can we compete effectively?
- Do we need to look for new markets?
- How are we going to raise finance?
- Will we be able to find enough trained employees?
- What is likely to happen in the economy?

Developing a strategy

Internal audit

People
Labour turnover
Motivation
Absenteeism
Productivity

Marketing
Sales
Advertising
Sales staff performance

Internal audit

Operations management
Productivity
Delivery
Stock control

Financial
Budgets and variances
Profitability
Cashflow
Investment appraisal

Figure 2 An internal audit

- An internal audit will be used to assess the strengths and weaknesses of the business.
- This is used to provide accurate information about each department.
- The best internal audits provide up-to-date accounting and statistical information: for example, cashflow forecast and labour turnover figures.
- The business needs to compare itself with its major competitors.

External audit

Technological change
Ethics
Competition
Pressure groups
EU
Culture ——— The business ——— Law
Environmental issues
Economic issues
Social issues
Customer bias
Political influences

Figure 3 An external audit

- The external audit looks at opportunities and threats in the external environment.
- Businesses need to be aware of the constantly changing environment in which they operate.
- The business then needs to consider the implications and take steps to deal with them.

The factors that affect a firm externally will be part of a PEST analysis.

- **Political.** Any of the actions of government can have an impact on a firm. This might be legislation on food hygiene or the movement of animals, tax changes or employment legislation.
- **Economic.** The economy is vitally important in the success of a business. Changes in the value of the currency, recessions and booms will all have an impact on demand and sales.
- **Social.** Changes in the characteristics and distribution of the population will influence a firm's sales and have an impact on the size and skills of the workforce. An increase in the number of young people going to university will improve the skills and qualifications of labour in the long term, but it might create a medium-term shortage of workers.
- **Technological.** Changes in technology offer the opportunity to improve efficiency, but they may also bring high investment costs and the threat of redundancy and discontent among employees. The introduction of more robotic assembly lines will be expensive. The result should be improved efficiency , but at a cost.

Other factors might include:

- **Competition.** The extent and success of the competition is always a potential threat for a business. A plan to open a new supermarket must take the existing competition into account.
- **Culture.** Businesses need to take account of the characteristics of their market and its needs. Changes in population must be taken account of in the range of goods that a business is selling.
- **Ethics.** Ethical behaviour is becoming increasingly important in the eyes of the consumer. The recent discussions on bankers' bonuses has shown how strongly the public will respond to perceived unethical behaviour.
- **Environment.** This already plays an important part in the operation of business and the economy. The need to be aware of environmental concerns is likely to increase as time goes on.

All of the information gained from these audits needs to be put into a SWOT analysis. This could be considered along with Ansoff's Matrix (see p. 16). The SWOT analysis must then be used to help with strategic planning for the future of the business.

Analysis

To achieve analysis it is possible to consider any of the elements that may affect a firm in relation to its future strategic plans. For example, having investigated the threat posed by competition, a business might decide to undertake market research to find a new niche in the market. This would be a costly exercise, but it could secure the business's profits as a result. Similarly, the expectation of a boom in demand could encourage a firm to undertake investment and training in order to improve efficiency.

Evaluation

Evaluation can be achieved by looking at the short and long-term effects of strategic planning or by considering and ranking a series of implications. For example, a firm might feel that there is going to be a decline in demand for its products as a result of its strategic planning. As a consequence, it might decide to allow natural wastage to reduce its workforce and delay decisions for expansion. These actions might help the business cope with the decline in demand in the long term, although the short-term implications, particularly among employees, might create problems.

Stakeholder objectives and strategic management

In any strategic management case study, it is essential to be able to consider how the various stakeholders of the business are affected by or can influence the business.

A stakeholder is a person or group of persons who is/are affected by the actions of the business.

OR

A stakeholder is a person or group of persons that may influence the actions of the business.

Most stakeholders will want the business to be a success (see below).

Typical stakeholders and their objectives

Stakeholder	Objectives
Owners/directors	Return on investment, profit via dividends, growth of the business, low costs
Employees	Job security, good pay and conditions, career progress
Customers	Good-quality products at reasonable prices, good customer service
Suppliers	Regular orders, good prices, prompt payment
Government	Good profits (taxable), high sales (more tax), stable prices (inflation), sales abroad (balance of payments), large number of employees (employment)
Banks	Prompt payments for borrowing, offer banking services for businesses
Local community	Jobs and therefore additional demand for goods and services

Many of the above stakeholders have matching objectives. The owners of the business want to see sales increase because this may lead to a higher level of profit, while employees will want sales to increase as this will provide a greater sense of security and an opportunity for higher wages.

However, there are frequently conflicts of objectives between stakeholders. Higher wages are an additional cost to the business that could reduce profits, and this would not be viewed favourably by the owners or the shareholders, as it would reduce dividends. Similarly, suppliers would welcome increased sales, but any attempt to reduce costs by negotiating lower prices from suppliers would not be welcomed by the latter.

The management of a business has to decide which stakeholder is more important at any given moment in time and act accordingly. However, the business will need to think long term as well as short term. Increasing investment expenditure will reduce the likelihood of increased profits in the short term. However, such investments will benefit shareholders in the long run.

Typical stakeholder conflicts

Business situation	Stakeholder conflicts
Increased desire for efficiency savings to remain competitive	**Shareholders** — happy as savings and remaining competitive will boost profits. **Employees** — less happy as efficiency savings may lead to job losses.
Increasing prices paid to suppliers	**Suppliers** — happy as revenue will increase if quantities purchased remain the same. **Customers** — less happy as they may have to pay more for the goods or services.
Increased production	**Employees** — happy as increased production enhances job security and may provide opportunities for overtime payments. **Local community** — less happy as increased production may mean additional pollution and traffic as goods are distributed. But some parts of the community may be happy, especially the local retailers.
Increased profits	**Shareholders** — may be happy if the profits are distributed, but less happy if the business decides to retain a significant proportion for investment. **Banks/lenders** — will not be as happy if profits are used for investment, as it is less likely the business will require a loan to finance the investment.
Reduction in waste and pollution	**Shareholders** — less happy in short term as costs will increase and therefore possibly reduce profits. Happy in long term as reputation of the business is increased, adding to sales and profits. **Local community** — happy as less pollution enhances the local environment. **Government** — happy as its targets for less landfill and reduced emissions more likely to be met. **Employees** — happy with improved working conditions, but less happy if savings are required to cover the additional costs of reducing waste and emissions, leading to redundancies.

There are no right answers to how management should decide its strategy to achieve any given objective. However, since 2006 there is a legal constraint that may influence how directors act.

The Companies Act (2006) requires directors to act in such a manner as to promote the success of the business and states that they should consider:

- the long-term consequences of their actions
- the interest of their employees and the company's relationships with its suppliers
- the impact of its operations on the local community and the environment

The legislation does not, however, solve the problem of conflicting objectives and the strategic management of the business. The three factors listed above are in themselves conflicting!

Analysis

Level 3 marks can be gained by ensuring that you offer implications of the strategy used by a business and its effects upon various stakeholders. It is important to spell out clearly what the implications are and how they will arise as a result of a specific strategy implemented by the business. Ensure that you select appropriate implications and ones that are likely to occur. In other words, try to be realistic in the context of the business and its situation as presented in the case material. You may also write about how a stakeholder will react.

Evaluation

Offering a judgement about which stakeholder will be affected the most is one route to Level 4 marks. It is again important for this module to consider the evidence in a balanced manner before reaching a judgement. Remember, there may be numbers available as evidence to help justify your ideas.

Market analysis

Knowledge of the market and of the needs of consumers is important for any business, especially when it wants to introduce a new product to the market.

Market research

Market research can be carried out by specialist firms, but the internet and improvements in communications have made it possible for firms to carry out their own research much more effectively. Information can be collected by using:

- feedback from sales staff on the state of the market and changes in consumer demand
- consumer focus groups
- internet market research
- online customer panels
- customer satisfaction questionnaires
- market research phone calls to customers
- specialist magazines

Market share

- Market share is the proportion of a market that is under the control of a business.
- In oligopoly, firms are often more concerned about market share in the short run than they are about profit.
- Market leadership has advantages for a business. It allows them to set the bar and influence consumer demand. It also puts them in a powerful position when negotiating with contractors.

Market size and growth

Market size can be measured by volume or sales value (turnover).

- Firms are interested in whether the market is growing or shrinking and what share of that market they control.
- A falling share of a shrinking market will need investigation and action.
- Market growth may come from a variety of sources. These may be improved living standards, population growth, changes in tastes or changes in expectations.
- Firms also need to be aware of the international market and changes in its size and characteristics.

The environment

Businesses also need to assess the environmental impact of their operations. The reasons for this are:

- the rapidly rising price of fuel and its effect on costs
- reducing a firm's carbon footprint can be a good marketing tool
- the need to comply with increasing legislation in this area, both in the UK and in the EU.

Analysis

It is possible to analyse by looking at the benefits that the firm will gain by monitoring its market. For example, if a business undertakes market research and finds that consumers would like some modifications made to a particular product, this will allow the firm to make the changes and increase revenue.

Evaluation

This could be achieved by looking at the place of market analysis in strategic planning. Market research is necessary when considering the opportunities for growth and diversification. By doing this research a business can assess the opportunities for the future and make strategic plans to move in the direction indicated as being most beneficial from the analysis undertaken.

Forecasting (time series analysis)

Time series analysis

Note: Now that there is a compulsory numerical question in this module, this is a concept that you need to know.

- Forecasting is the use of existing data to predict future trends. One method of doing this is **time series analysis**.
- Although this technique can be used to forecast any data, it is frequently used to forecast sales.
- The technique is sometimes referred to as 'moving average'.
- The forecast is based on past data.
- Time series analysis combines the moving average of past data over a given period of time to project figures for the future.
- The technique assumes that past data can be used to predict for the future, which is open to debate.

The trend and fluctuations

Figures fluctuate over time, especially for seasonal products and services. The **trend** will smooth out these fluctuations. Establishing whether the trend is upwards or downwards will allow the business to respond accordingly.

- **Cyclical fluctuations** are variations related to the business cycle/economic cycle such as the recession that has led to a fall in demand for many consumer goods.
- **Seasonal fluctuations** are changes in figures during any given year. How much a business is affected will depend upon the nature of the product or service. Agriculture and tourism are more seasonal than the demand for shoes.
- **Random fluctuations** refer to changes in the level of sales that are not easy to predict. The weather can greatly influence sales of many items and therefore make forecasts much more difficult.

Calculations

Although it is very important to be able to undertake the required calculations, it is of greater significance that you are able to use the information in an appropriate manner.

Calculating a three-period average

Year	Sales (£000)	Three-period total (£000)	Three-period average (moving average) (£000)
2000	110		
2001	106	336 (A) (110 + 106 + 120)	112 (A) (336/3)
2002	120	356 (B) (106 + 120 + 130)	118.6 (B) (356/3)
2003	130	375	125
2004	125	395	131.6
2005	140	415	138.3
2006	150	450	150
2007	160	450	150
2008	140		
2009	130		
2010	132		

When calculating the three-period average, it is important to ensure that you are careful when adding up the three chosen years. You are allowed a calculator in the exam.

Note that the answer for the three-period total and average is placed in the middle of the period. Therefore the three-period total for the first 3 years is placed in the middle year, which is 2001.

The process is the same regardless of the units for the period.

Try for yourself to calculate:
(a) the 3-period total for 2008–10
(b) the 3-period average for 2008–10

The answers are given at the bottom of the page. Remember to show your workings.

If you plot the sales figures on to a graph, instead of joining up all the dots, you can draw a straight line to represent the **line of best fit** (see Figure 4). This represents the overall trend and can be used to predict future sales by extrapolating (in simple terms, extending the line of best fit).

(a) 2008–10 total = 140 + 130 + 132 = 402
(b) 2008–10 average = 402/3 = 134

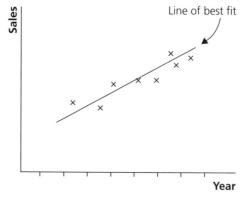

Figure 4 Line of best fit

Calculating the cyclical variation

Cyclical variation is the difference between the actual sales figures and the moving average.

Note that it is the actual figure that determines whether the answer is positive or negative. If the actual figure is less than the moving average, the cyclical variation is negative.

Year	Sales (£000)	Three-period total (£000)	Three-period average (moving average) (£000)	Cyclical variation (actual figure – moving average) (£000)
2000	110 ⎫			
2001	106 ⎬A ⎫	336 (A) (110 + 106 + 120)	112 (A) (336/3)	106 − 112 = −6
2002	120 ⎭ ⎬B	356 (B) (106 + 120 + 130)	118.6 (B) (356/3)	+1.4
2003	130 ⎭	375	125	+5
2004	125	395	131.6	−6.6
2005	140	415	138.3	
2006	150	450	150	
2007	160	450	150	
2008	140			
2009	130			
2010	132			

From the cyclical variation it is possible to go on and calculate the average cyclical variation by taking the cyclical variations for all three figures in the three-period time and dividing by 3.

You might want to try and calculate the cyclical variations for each year from 2005 to 2010.

Limitations of forecasting

- Forecasts are only as reliable as the data used.
- Past data will not necessarily reflect future figures, as circumstances change.
- This technique cannot distinguish between old and new data (the latest data being the most reliable).
- The objectives of the business are not considered. Hence you will need to think carefully about such objectives when using the data.

Analysis

The obvious route into Level 3 marks is to offer implications of the figures calculated. These will need to be in the context of the case and if possible noting the objectives of the business concerned. For example, establishing that the overall trend is upwards means that it will be easier for the business to achieve its objective of increased profitability. This is because the forecast increase in sales should reduce unit costs and, assuming the profitability of the sales is similar, lead to an increased level of profits.

Evaluation

This can be achieved by commenting on the limitations of the data and hence the degree of reliability. Much will depend upon the source and date of the data and the period of time for which the forecast is made. Suggesting which part of the business will be affected most by the figures is another obvious way to gain Level 4 marks. Noting the type of product or service will also help you to make valid points about cyclical and/or seasonal variations and the consequent reliability of the data.

Decision trees

A **decision tree** is a technique that can be used as part of the decision making process. If there are options that a business can pursue, it can be used to assess the 'best' option, based on probabilities and monetary returns.

Decision trees are visual and therefore easier to comprehend and utilise.

Key symbols

Tip If you are asked to draw a decision tree, get the diagram right before putting in any numbers.

Two key parts are required for using decision trees:
- probabilities (P) of an outcome (representing the risk). The total of the probabilities will always add up to 1
- estimated monetary reward (EMV) for an option (reward)

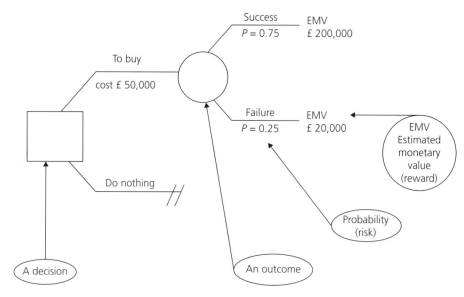

Figure 5 Decision trees

Drawing the decision tree

- Always start with a decision (square).
- After a decision, what are the options or outcomes (circles)?
- Clearly label the options with probabilities and EMVs.
- Put in the costs of a decision.
- A 2p coin is perfect for drawing the circles, leaving sufficient room for numbers to be inserted.

Once a tree has been drawn and carefully labelled (this is essential if marks are to be gained), the calculations can be undertaken.

Calculating the expected values

Using Figure 6 (see overleaf):
- Calculations are made from right to left on the tree.
- Expected value = EMV × probability [A]
- Add outcomes (options). [B]
- Put expected value into the circle. [C]
- Subtract the cost of the option. [D]
- Select the higher figure to place in the decision square. [E]

Notice how in Figure 6, the layout shows clearly how the calculations have been done. If you do this, any errors you make in the calculations will mean that there is still an opportunity for you to score well.

From the figure it is clear that investing in a new packaging machine is better than buying a second-hand machine (£235,000 compared with £176,000). Although the new machine is a better option according to the decision tree, however, there may be other factors to consider. These can be extracted from the case.

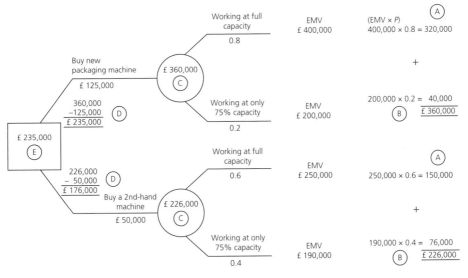

Figure 6 Decision tree: example

Good candidates may ask why the EMV on the option to buy the new machine that is operating at 75% capacity is so much lower than the EMV while operating at full capacity.

Reasons may be sought as to why the machines would be operating at only 75%.

It is perfectly acceptable and indeed encouraged for candidates to think of other factors, such as the condition of the second-hand machine, the amount of maintenance that it will require and therefore the time when it will not be productive (downtime), and the life of the machine when compared to the new one.

Other considerations

Other considerations include:
- amount of finance available
- viability of borrowing finance
- which option best suits the objectives of the business
- state of the business environment
- rate of return/payback of the chosen option
- accuracy of data

Benefits of decision trees

- They are a simple method of deciding which option to undertake.
- As they are visual, it is easy to 'see' the answer and the options.
- There is an attempt to 'calculate' the risk involved.
- They are quick to apply.

Limitations of decision trees

- Reliability of data is an issue.
- Source and accuracy of probability figures are problematic (forecast only).
- EMV figures involve estimates of sales revenues and costs.
- The time period over which figures are based needs to be taken into account.
- No real qualitative factors are included.

Although there are obvious limitations to the technique, it is a useful additional decision-making tool for a business to use.

Decision trees in the examination

Given the time constraint, it is likely that you will be asked to use a decision tree rather than having to draw one. However, it is vital that you can draw a decision tree and it will help your understanding of the technique.

You may be given additional information within the question that will affect the tree or the calculations. Your teacher will help you prepare if it is clear that a decision tree is to be included from the information in the pre-issued case.

Analysis

A typical question may ask you to recommend which machine the business should buy. The analysis will consider the implications for the business of buying one of the two options available in the context of its situation, its objectives and 'other' factors.

If the business bought the new machine, the life expectancy ought to be longer and therefore less would need to be spent on maintenance. Consequently, there would be less downtime and the machine would be more productive. This would enable the business to meet its orders and expand, while keeping its unit costs down.

It is important that the analysis is laid out, step by step, rather than making a huge leap by suggesting that the new machine is better because it is more productive. This alone would not gain a Level 3 mark.

Evaluation

A justified judgement needs to be made in the context of the case and the question.

A good answer would 'weigh' the evidence using not only the decision tree but also other techniques, such as payback if possible, along with other considerations. Once the evidence has been considered, you will need to recommend which option is the most appropriate in the present situation for this business. This is also the right time to indicate any assumptions you have made and/or to acknowledge the limitations of the data. Nevertheless, you are expected to use the case material to justify your view.

Measures of business performance (people)

Businesses need to be able to measure the performance of their workforce in a variety of areas. The main measures are productivity, absenteeism and labour turnover.

Productivity

- Productivity is output per worker and it measures the efficiency of the workforce.
- Most businesses want to increase productivity if possible because it will lower the cost per unit.
- New production techniques, such as kaizen, have improved labour productivity.

$$productivity = \frac{total\ output}{number\ of\ employees}$$

For example, if a business employs 8 people and total output per week is 12,000 units, productivity is 12,000/8, which is 1,500 units per week.

Absenteeism

- Absenteeism may give an indication of worker morale and job satisfaction.
- It is calculated by looking at the number of working days lost across the whole business as a percentage of the total possible days worked.

$$absenteeism\ rate = \frac{no.\ of\ days\ lost\ through\ absence}{total\ possible\ days\ worked} \times 100$$

For example, if a firm employs 20 workers who work a 5-day week for 45 weeks of the year, the total possible days worked are $20 \times 45 \times 5 = 4,500$ days.

Over the past year, 100 days were lost through absence.

$$absenteeism\ rate = (100/4,500) \times 100 = 2.2\%$$

The factors that contribute to absenteeism are:
- lack of job satisfaction
- work that is not challenging
- poor management
- stress
- problems in workplace relationships
- lack of recognition
- poor working conditions

Some absenteeism is inevitable, but it imposes costs on the business in terms of covering the work, lost orders and poor customer relations.

Tip Think about the lack of motivational factors as a good source of explanation for high absenteeism.

Solutions for reducing absenteeism

- Management can actively manage absence by giving 'return to work' interviews after a period of absence to find the causes.
- Managers need to ensure that workers have the training to do the job effectively.
- Work should not be boring or lack challenge. Job rotation or cell working can help with this.
- Incentives can be offered to improve attendance.

Labour turnover

Labour turnover is another quantifiable measure that gives an indication of performance. However, it should not be viewed in isolation. It is also important to take account of the fact that some areas, like catering, always have higher rates of turnover than elsewhere in the economy.

$$\text{labour turnover} = \frac{\text{no. of people leaving in a period}}{\text{average number of workers in that period}} \times 100$$

For example, if 20 workers leave a business in a year and the average number of workers during that year has been 300, the labour turnover is (20/300) × 100 = 6.7%.

Costs and causes of labour turnover

Losing workers and recruiting new ones imposes costs on a business. Some labour turnover is to be expected, but if the rate is high or starts to increase, managers should be concerned and start to investigate the causes.

The reasons for high or increasing labour turnover might be as follows:

- The recruitment process might be at fault. It is possible that job adverts are attracting the 'wrong' candidates.
- The induction process might be inadequate, leaving workers feeling unsure of their role.
- The job itself might lack the necessary challenge and variety.
- The pay rates may be lower than those paid elsewhere in the region, leaving workers feeling a sense of grievance.
- Skill shortages in a certain area might lead to higher than usual turnover.

Analysis

It is possible to analyse problems in any area of performance by looking at their effects on the costs of the firm. For example, if a business is experiencing higher labour turnover than previously, this should be investigated by management. If managers can find the reason, this will reduce the business's labour costs and may result in better motivation and higher productivity.

Evaluation

Evaluation can be achieved by looking at the long-term strategic benefits of taking short- and medium-term action on issues like high absenteeism or low productivity. For example, if managers try to improve productivity by introducing job enrichment or rotation, they should begin to see improved motivation. Hopefully this will lead to higher productivity and lower costs for the business in the long term. All of this would help to achieve a strategic objective of growth.

The nature of economic activity

What is 'the economy'?

'The economy' is not one single unit. It refers to the combined actions of:
- **people** acting both as wage-earning employees and as consumers
- the activities (i.e. the production and employment decisions) of all the **different businesses in the UK**
- **the government**, which is a major provider of goods and services — these have to be financed through taxation and borrowing
- **economies abroad**, which affect the UK economy through trading relationships.

Tip Although a clear understanding of macroeconomic issues is essential, examiners are not looking for detailed, technical explanations of how the economy works. It is much more important for you to be able to analyse how the economic environment affects the strategic behaviour of a particular business.

What is 'economic activity'?

'Economic activity' refers to the production of goods and services. This production can be primary, secondary or tertiary. Economic activity refers to what is happening to output in all of these sectors.

A term often used when considering economic activity is **gross domestic product (GDP)**, where 'gross' means 'total', 'domestic' means 'in the UK' and 'product' means 'output'. Rising GDP is advantageous. This is because:
- UK firms benefit from the growth. When spending is rising, the demand for products and services will be rising too. This will hopefully mean more profit — some of which can be used for further business expansion and development.
- Employment will be rising as firms will need to employ more people in order to meet the demand for products. Jobs are more likely to be secure when GDP is rising.
- The government should also be pleased with rising GDP, as the rise in economic activity means more tax revenue from both people and businesses.

All of this is true in reverse: that is, generally speaking, a fall in GDP is not good for businesses, people or the government.

Factors that affect economic activity

The easiest way to consider how the economy operates is the **circular flow of income**, where the economy is divided into two groups: households and firms. In households, people earn income by going to work. They then spend that income, thus generating a flow of income in the opposite direction.

However, not all income earned flows back to UK businesses. Some is taken in tax, some is saved and some is spent on imports. These are known as **leakages** from the circular flow. In general, leakages reduce the level of economic activity.

On the other hand, some income flows to UK firms from sources other than the consumer. Investment (the purchase of buildings and machinery) comes from other firms, the government spends a lot of money, and consumers abroad buy our exports. These sources are known as **injections** into the circular flow. In general, injections increase the level of economic activity.

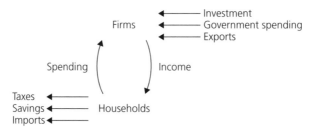

Figure 7 The circular flow of income

The circular flow of income is a continuous process. As long as consumer spending plus the three injections are sufficient for businesses to sell all of their products, the level of GDP and the level of employment will remain unchanged.

What happens if leakages are not equal to injections?

There is no reason why the total amount of leakages from the economy should be the same as the total amount of injections.

- **If injections of income are greater than the amount of withdrawals, then the level of economic activity will rise.** This should be beneficial; as spending increases, businesses will employ more workers.
- **If withdrawals of income are greater than injections, the level of economic activity will fall.** Spending will fall, demand will fall and businesses will make employees redundant, will invest less, or may (if the fall is large enough) be forced to close.

Economic policy (see pp. 40–43) is not about trying to get injections and withdrawals to balance to the last pound — or even the last £10 billion. Economic policy is about establishing an economic environment within which businesses can prosper and grow. This means that policy-makers are trying to prevent the harmful effects of either a sudden large rise in the circular flow of income (which could mean inflation and/or a worsening of the balance of trade) or a huge fall (which will slow GDP and cause unemployment to rise).

Analysis

A comment could be made about how and why a business will be affected, positively or negatively, by a change in the level of economic activity caused by one or more leakage or injection. Alternatively, you could consider how the business in the case may react to this.

Evaluation

When evaluating the likely effects of a change in economic activity on a business, it is useful to use the mnemonic 'TED':

T — the **trend** in the change

E — the **extent** of the change

D — the likely **duration** of the change

- **T.** If GDP has fallen over the past 6 months, another quarterly fall may not be unexpected as it is part of a trend. A business may well already have anticipated it and adjusted output, employment and investment plans accordingly. On the other hand, if the fall comes unexpectedly and is against the trend, this may cause more of an upset.
- **E.** How large was the fall? A 0.1% fall is far less serious than a 1% fall. If it was 0.1%, then although there has been 'a fall in GDP', this may not have a very large effect on the business.
- **D.** Businesses are likely to consider how long the fall will last. If it is expected to be short term, it will have little effect. On the other hand, if economists are predicting a prolonged drop in GDP, a firm's reactions will be different.

Therefore a small fall in line with the trend, which is expected to reverse shortly, will have much less effect on the strategic decisions of businesses than a large fall against the trend, which is expected to last for a long time.

The economic cycle

What is 'the economic cycle'?

The long-term trend rate of GDP in a developed western economy is upward. Nevertheless economic activity proceeds in cycles: sometimes GDP is rising and sometimes it is falling. It does not follow the actual path of the trend. These rises and falls follow a pattern of different stages that can be identified as boom, recession, slump and recovery. Where the economy is on the cycle, and how long each stage lasts, is of considerable importance to a business.

The economic cycle (also called 'the business cycle') is usually represented as follows:

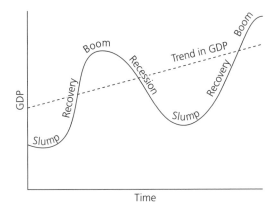

Figure 8 The four stages of the economic cycle

What happens in each stage of the cycle?

Boom

Businesses are profitable and feeling confident about future sales. There will be a high level of employment, consumption and therefore demand for products. This confidence will encourage businesses to invest in new plant and machinery. Investment is an injection into the circular flow of income (see p. 34) and will lead to a further rise in GDP. The boom eventually reaches a peak (sometimes called 'the ceiling') and GDP will not rise any further in that cycle.

Recession

A recession is two successive quarterly falls in GDP. In a recession, sales fall and thus business confidence (about future consumer demand) also falls. Businesses lay off employees, which causes consumer spending to fall further. This in turn lowers demand and profits, which is likely to reduce investment. A recession may only affect certain parts of the economy: for example, the recession in the early 1980s affected the 'heavy' industries of the north much more than businesses in the south of the UK.

Slump

A slump (also known as 'a trough') is similar to a recession except that the features are more serious and widespread; instead of affecting a few sectors of the economy, all of the economy is affected.

Recovery

Economic activity starts to rise. Consumers start to spend again and demand increases. Business confidence starts to rise as profits rise. Firms begin to invest again and recruit more employees. Higher employment increases consumer spending and this, combined with rising investment, leads to the start of a new cycle.

Tip You will not be asked to explain why the economic cycle exists (although you should have some knowledge of this), and any question in the examination will centre on one specific business, not all of the businesses in the economy. Therefore focus your analysis and evaluation on how the specific firm in the case study will be affected by each stage of the cycle.

Why is the economic cycle important to a business?

The economic cycle is a very powerful determinant of consumer demand. If GDP is predicted to fall steadily for the next 12 months, demand in the economy will fall — but not all businesses will be affected in the same way. It is necessary to consider the extent to which a particular business's products are essential for everyday life. If the product is considered essential, such as food, then a recession may have little effect on demand — although it is likely that the retailer will now order more 'value'-type products. On the other hand, a business selling luxury items like wide-screen televisions and top-of-the-range hi-fi equipment is likely to see a large drop in sales.

A business needs to know where the economy is on the cycle in order to plan ahead and make long-term decisions about output. And if a recession is predicted, for example, the firm's decisions about output also mean making decisions about other business areas:

- **Staffing.** Making employees redundant can be costly and can lower morale. In addition, if competent employees are laid off, how easy will it be to recruit ones of a similar calibre when the recession is over?
- **Investment.** If investment in new technology is cancelled, will the business be at a disadvantage in the future compared to others at home and abroad?
- **Marketing.** Should marketing expenditure be cut back to save money at a time when sales and therefore profit may be falling? If this occurs, what are the long-term implications for market share, brand loyalty and therefore sales?

Where on the economic cycle?

A business might evaluate where the economy is on the economic cycle by using:

- output/sales trends from the business's own factory(ies)/shop(s)
- competitors' report and accounts
- the trend in GDP
- the trend in national employment and spending levels.

Analysis

Analysis should consider the implication of each stage of the cycle for a business's sales. If there is a recession, for example, it is likely that many businesses will see sales fall and this may cause cashflow problems. The reaction to this will need to be carefully planned.

It is essential to form a judgement on *the extent* to which the demand for the business's product(s) is likely to be affected at each stage of the economic cycle. Remember 'TED' (p. 35): if after years of growth (T), a small (E) and short-lived (D) decline in GDP is predicted, this is likely to have relatively minor effect on a business's strategic (human resource, financial, production and marketing) plans.

An alternative route into Level 4 would be to make a judgement as to *how* a business should adapt to a change in the state of the economy. Should it reduce output and lower staff costs? Or should it try actively to raise the level of demand for its products by advertising more? Should it do both? Might it be possible to try to sell (more) abroad? The more strategic your approach is to questions such as these, the higher your mark will be.

The macroeconomic objectives of government

A government has four macroeconomic objectives:

- **a low and stable rate of inflation** — in 2003 the government set a target of 2% a year for the rate at which prices in the economy should increase
- **a high level of employment** — as many people as possible should be in work
- **economic growth** — there should be an increase in the amount of goods and services produced in the economy each year
- **a balance of payments equilibrium** — the value of exports should be broadly similar to the value of imports

The achievement of these objectives is important if businesses are to succeed.

A low and stable rate of inflation

Inflation is **a persistent tendency for prices to rise**. A high rate of inflation is bad for the economy and therefore bad for businesses.

- **Inflation makes UK goods uncompetitive.** The world economy is globalised; identical products (e.g. the same brand of televisions, computers and freezers) can be made anywhere in the world. If the UK's rate of inflation is higher than the rates in other countries, the price of UK exports will rise. This will make them less attractive to consumers abroad. Furthermore, if prices of home-produced goods are rising fast, UK consumers will prefer to buy cheaper foreign imports instead of those made by UK businesses.
- **Inflation can affect investment.** A multinational company will want to locate and produce in the cheapest possible location so as to maximise profits. This means considering where costs are lowest — and likely to stay low. A country where inflation is high and where the price of labour and raw materials is rising

steeply is not attractive. If inflation was high in the UK, it would deter investment and lead to higher unemployment.

Tip Remember, when inflation falls this does not mean that prices have gone down; it just means that **the rate of increase** in prices has fallen.

A high level of employment

Unemployment means that some workers who want jobs cannot find them; there is an excess supply of labour. It may be true that this benefits some firms as labour costs may fall; however, there are a number of reasons to be concerned about unemployment.

- **Unemployment is a waste of human resources.** If the unemployed were at work, businesses would be producing more goods and services. We would all have more goods and services to buy.
- **Unemployment is bad for the individual.** Unemployment is often associated with social problems such as drug taking and low self-esteem.
- **Unemployment is bad for society as a whole.** The problems associated with unemployment must be paid for. In addition, benefits have to be paid to those without a job. 'Society' has to pay, in the sense that this money could be spent on other things such as the environment or education.

Economic growth

- If GDP is rising, more goods and services are produced and businesses are more profitable because spending rises. The number of people in work rises and people have a higher standard of living. Tax revenue for the government will also rise if the economy is growing.
- Modern thinking is not only that we need growth, but that growth should be **sustainable**; it should come from using renewable resources, and with as little damage to the environment as possible. Businesses adopting an approach that does this can use it as a marketing advantage.

A balance of payments equilibrium

The balance of payments is the term used to describe the financial records of the UK's trade with the rest of the world. The most important component of it is the **balance of trade** — the record of the UK's imports and exports. It is this figure that usually appears in the news as the 'headline' figure. An excess of imports over exports is a **trade deficit**. An excess of exports over imports is a **trade surplus**.

A trade deficit is bad for businesses because:
- UK businesses are 'losing out' on sales to foreign firms because of consumers buying imports.
- UK businesses are not earning sufficient revenue from exports to pay for the country's volume of imports.

The balance of trade is important because imports have to be paid for. It is important that the UK exports sufficient quantities of products to 'pay its way' internationally. If a person spends more than he or she receives in income, at first his or her savings will be run down and then, if the pattern of earning and spending continues, he or she will have to borrow. This cannot continue for ever. It is the same principle for a country.

Analysis

At different times a government may place more emphasis on one objective than another. If inflation is rising, the Bank of England may raise the rate of interest to slow it down. This, however, will negatively affect the level of employment. Thus, if reference is made in the case study to 'fears of inflation in the economy', you should consider the likely policy measures that might be adopted and hence the effect of these on the business.

Evaluation

Although you should have a broad understanding of the macroeconomic objectives, why they are important and the policies used to bring them about, you will not be asked 'technical' economic questions about them.

Evaluative comments could be based on the likely consequences for the business of the government choosing to prioritise a particular objective and the policies it chooses to use to achieve it. A business's strategic response to these policies will need to consider the nature of the product(s) it sells, and a judgement will need to be made on the extent to which it is likely to be affected. Consider the 'TED' framework again (see p. 35).

Economic policy and its effect on businesses

The economic policy, or policies, that are used at a particular time depend on what economic objective(s) the government or the Bank of England is trying to achieve. Economic policy is conducted in three ways: through **monetary policy**, **fiscal policy** and the **exchange rate** (see p. 43).

Monetary policy

Monetary policy — conducted by the Monetary Policy Committee of the Bank of England (MPC) — is concerned with varying the level of demand in the economy through the rate of interest, in order to meet the government's target of 2% inflation in the economy.

The rate of interest is 'the price of money'. The price of any product affects its demand, and similarly the demand for money will respond to changes in the rate of interest. When the Bank of England changes the rate of interest, the commercial (i.e. high street) banks have to follow suit. If the Bank of England wants consumers and businesses to spend less, it raises the rate of interest. The commercial banks in turn increase their rates. This will discourage borrowing and spending by both consumers and businesses. It may also encourage some people who have surplus cash to save — this also lowers spending. The opposite would apply if the bank cut the rate.

There are three effects of an interest rate change on a business:
- **The effect(s) arising from the change in the demand for its products.** If the rate rises, consumer spending will fall. This is because the interest payable on mortgages, other loans and credit cards will increase, and so spending on other products will fall — especially luxury items, which are often bought on credit. There is also an effect on saving: people without loans may now save more and this will also reduce overall consumption.
- **The effect(s) arising from the change in borrowing costs.** A lot of investment is made with borrowed money. If the rate rises, investment will fall. Businesses are more likely to continue to use older machinery for as long as they can because the cost of borrowing money to replace it has risen. In addition, businesses know that a rise in the rate will slow down consumer spending — this will make it even less attractive to invest.
- **The effect(s) arising from the change in the exchange rate.** If the rate rises, the exchange rate is likely to rise too. The pound is now a more attractive currency to invest in, as the return on deposits of sterling has gone up. The increased demand for pounds will cause the exchange rate to rise. This affects any business selling abroad: it will find that its exports become more expensive to foreign customers. It also means that a business that imports raw materials will find that they have become cheaper (see pp. 43–46).

The opposite would apply if the rate of interest fell.

> **Tip** It is worth remembering that changes in interest rates have a dual effect: on consumer demand and also on the firm in terms of how much it costs to service any debts it has. An answer that analyses and evaluates the effects of both of these factors will be stronger than an answer that deals only with one.

Fiscal policy

Fiscal policy aims to alter the total level of demand in the economy. It operates through taxation and government spending, and is controlled by the government not the Bank of England.

Taxation

Cuts in taxes encourage spending. If income tax (or VAT) is cut, consumers will spend more. If corporation tax is cut, companies keep more of their profits and will spend more on investment and/or distribute more profit to shareholders as dividends — which is likely to increase consumer spending. These measures will boost the level of economic activity. The reverse is true.

Taxes have other uses as well:

- **To raise revenue.** The government can then spend this on schools, hospitals, roads, etc.
- **To influence the pattern of expenditure.** Through different rates of taxation the government encourages certain types of consumption (e.g. liquefied petroleum gas (LPG) has a lower rate of tax than petrol) and discourages others (high rates of tax are placed on cigarettes and alcohol).

Public spending

Public spending is not to be confused with 'spending by the public'. The government can strongly influence the level of consumer demand by varying its own spending. If the amount of government spending rises, this will increase the level of economic activity and more jobs will be created. The reverse is also true.

In summary, rises in GDP will be caused by the following economic policies:

- a cut in the rate of interest
- a cut in tax rates
- an increase in government spending (public spending)

Falls in GDP will be caused by the following economic policies:

- a rise in the rate of interest
- a rise in tax rates
- a reduction in government spending.

The multiplier effect

If a business experiences a change in the demand for its products, this will have an additional (i.e. multiplier) effect on its suppliers. For example, the recession resulting from the credit crunch reduced the demand for new houses and this fall in demand caused a negative multiplier effect. Builders ordered less of all kinds of materials, from bricks to baths, from their suppliers. This sort of effect happened in many industries and GDP fell in businesses of all kinds across the economy. The multiplier also works positively as well; when GDP rises, all sorts of businesses benefit as the gains from the growth are 'multiplied' across different sectors.

Analysis

Analysis can be demonstrated by showing the consequences for the business in the case study of a change in economic policy.

Evaluation

To help you, there is a comprehensive section for evaluation on this topic. 'TED' (mentioned on p. 35) is absolutely essential when evaluating the likely effects of any change in economic policy on a business's strategy. Remember that this means:

T — the **trend** in the variable

E — the **extent** of the change

D — the **duration** of the change

Consider a question concerning the effects of a rise in government spending.

- **T.** Assume that a government has been in power for 2 years. If public spending has been increased in the last two budgets, the latest rise will not be unexpected — and indeed it is likely that the government may have announced it in advance. A business may also already have anticipated it. This may mean that it has an advertising campaign and a series of 'special offers' ready to be launched to try to tap into the increase in income that will result.
- **E.** The extent of the increase is important. A rise of £1 billion is insignificant, but a rise of £50 billion is not. How large is the increase and is it in line with the trend rate of growth in public spending?
- **D.** Businesses will consider how long the new level of spending can be sustained. If it is expected to be short term (due to the state of the government's finances) then businesses may well reason that demand will not actually rise by very much in the longer term and the policy may therefore have little effect on investment. After all, why build new factories equipped with the latest technology if the demand is not going to be there to purchase the output? If, however, it is expected that the rise will not be reversed for a year or more, reactions could be very different.

Therefore a small rate rise in public spending, below its trend rate of growth, which is expected to be reversed shortly, is indeed 'a rise in public spending'. But it will have much less effect on strategic decision making than an above-the-trend rise accompanied by the chancellor publishing figures showing that the government's finances are in great shape and stating that public spending will remain high for the rest of the parliament.

This TED approach can also be used with changes in any instruments of economic policy, such as income tax, VAT, interest rates and exchange rates.

The exchange rate

The exchange rate is the value of the pound in terms of another currency. Currencies are traded in a market — the global foreign exchange market. Like the situation in any market, the price of the pound (i.e. the rate of exchange) is determined by the demand for, and the supply of, pounds in the market.

Effects on business of a change in the exchange rate

A fall in the exchange rate
- The pound will buy a smaller amount of foreign currency than before (the pound is 'worth less').

- UK exports become cheaper for foreign buyers.
- Imports into the UK become more expensive.

A rise in the exchange rate
- The pound will buy a larger amount of foreign currency than before (the pound is 'worth more').
- UK exports become more expensive to foreign buyers.
- Imports into the UK become cheaper.

Economic policy and the exchange rate

The exchange rate can be used as an economic policy tool to help increase employment and growth or to reduce inflation.

Employment
A lower rate of exchange can help to increase economic activity.
- A lower rate will make UK exports cheaper.
- This should increase the demand for exports.
- As exports are an injection of income, this in turn should create employment and economic growth.

Inflation
A higher rate of exchange can be part of a policy to combat inflation.
- Imports of raw materials and equipment become cheaper.
- This helps UK businesses to keep costs and therefore prices down.

The rate of interest and the rate of exchange

In order to understand how the exchange rate is used to influence the economy, it is necessary to understand **'hot money'**. This is the term given to the flow of money from country to country, which is chasing the highest rate of interest it can get. If UK rates of interest are higher than those in other countries, foreign banks will take advantage of this. They will use their foreign currency to demand pounds, which they will then deposit in UK banks. This increased demand for pounds will raise the price of pounds: that is, the exchange rate.

Alternatively, if UK banks think that the rate of interest in (say) the USA is very attractive compared to the rate in the UK, they will supply pounds and buy dollars. This increased supply of pounds will lower the rate of exchange.

Changes in the rate of interest therefore affect the exchange rate via flows of 'hot money' and are a major determinant of the exchange rate.
- If the Bank of England wants the exchange rate to rise, it can put up the rate of interest.
- This makes the return on deposits of money in the UK more attractive. Hot money will flow into the UK and the rate of exchange will rise.

- Alternatively, if the bank wants the rate of exchange to fall, it can lower the rate of interest.
- This makes the return on deposits of money in the UK less attractive. Hot money will flow out of the UK and the rate of exchange will fall.

Effects on businesses of a change in the exchange rate

A UK business that imports but does not export

If the rate rises, this means that imported inputs are now cheaper, so the firm is now faced with the dilemma of:

- giving customers a price cut if this will generate extra sales (i.e. demand is price elastic)
- taking a larger profit margin — the business may simply be thankful for the cost reduction and take the extra profit per item

If the rate falls, the cost of the imported inputs will have risen. The business is now faced with:

- passing the cost increase on to the customers — will this be possible?
- absorbing the increase in costs and accepting lower profits

A UK business that exports but does not import

If the rate rises, although the price in pounds is unchanged, the foreign currency price has risen. The firm is now faced with:

- the likelihood of selling less abroad
- trying to increase UK sales to offset fewer sales abroad
- trying to lower costs and therefore the selling price to offset the rise in the exchange rate

If the rate falls, although the price in pounds is unchanged, the foreign currency price has now fallen. The business is now faced with the dilemma of:

- charging a higher foreign currency price and increasing the profit per item
- leaving the sterling price unchanged and hoping that those abroad will increase their demand

A UK business that both imports and exports

A business may well import various components and raw materials and then assemble them into a finished product which is then exported. Whether a change in the exchange rate is beneficial or not depends on the relative magnitude of the two effects.

If the rate falls:

- Exports are now cheaper abroad as the foreign currency price has fallen.
- More goods should now be sold abroad.
- However, any imports that the business uses have now become more expensive.
- If these are passed on to the customer, it will mean a rise in the final selling price and demand may fall.

If the rate rises:

- Imported components and raw materials are now cheaper for the UK firm.
- However, despite the lower cost of components and materials, the rise in the rate raises the foreign currency selling price of the product.
- As a result, fewer products may be sold abroad.

There is not going to be an exchange rate which is satisfactory for all UK businesses. Whether a rate change is beneficial depends on a variety of factors, such as:

- does the firm import components/raw materials — if so, what proportion of total costs do these account for?
- if imported component prices rise, can substitutes from the UK be used instead?
- does the firm export products — if so, what proportion of total sales do these account for?
- how price elastic is the product — can cost increases be passed on?

A consideration of these issues would be useful in evaluating the effect of a rate change.

Analysis

The exchange rate has consequences for most UK businesses and these need to be considered carefully in the above manner. However, it is only one (albeit a very important one) of a variety of reasons determining if a product is bought from a particular business in a particular country. Other issues, such as reliability, quality, marketing and loyalty, will also determine consumption patterns and will need to be analysed (and evaluated) when considering a firm's strategic response to a rate change.

Evaluation

To gain evaluation marks, you need to be able to form a judgement on the extent to which a particular business may be affected. The 'TED' framework (p. 35) can be applied again here.

Trend. If the rate fall is part of a trend and this had been expected, it may have little effect on a business's strategy.

Extent. Small changes in the value of the pound occur every day. How large was the change? A small change will have less impact on strategic planning than a large one — especially if the change is expected to be short lived (see below).

Duration. Is the rate change expected to be temporary or more permanent? A fall in the rate makes exports cheaper, but a business will be foolish to restructure production in order to try to sell more abroad unless it is sure that the pound will not rise steeply and cause the price of exports to rise again.

A small change, in line with the trend, which is not expected to last long, will have a minimal impact on a firm's decisions compared with a large, unexpected change of uncertain duration.

content guidance

The European Union

The European Union (EU) is a group of countries aiming to improve the standard of living for their citizens by adopting common economic and social policies. In 2010 there were 27 members.

Free trade and the EU

Trade brings several benefits:
- Consumers benefit from a greater variety of goods and services.
- Firms can gain economies of scale.
- Workers have improved employment opportunities.

One of the major goals of the EU is to create a large market where member states can trade freely with each other to gain these benefits. This means that they do not impose trade restrictions such as quotas or tariffs on each other's products. These measures invite retaliation and lead to less trade taking place.

The term **single market** is often used when discussing the EU. As well as working to remove tariffs and quotas, this means that businesses in the member countries trade with a single set of rules on the movement of goods, finance and people, rather than having different ones for each country, which would complicate and therefore discourage trade. Free trade and the single market make trade easier, and so businesses can prosper.

Implications of the single market for UK businesses

There are three main benefits:
- It offers access to hundreds of millions of new consumers.
- A business exporting to EU countries as well as operating in the UK can gain economies of scale. These are the advantages in terms of lower unit costs that come from large-scale production. Lower costs per item mean a larger profit margin.
- Selling in the EU can help a business's stability. It no longer has 'all its eggs in one (UK) basket'.

There are also disadvantages:
- Competition is not all 'one way': EU firms can take UK businesses' customers away. UK firms must fight to be efficient, especially against the low-cost firms from the newly joined eastern European members.
- The cost of complying with EU laws and the set-up costs of starting to export (see next page) may be considerable.

Implications for a UK business of exporting to the EU

'Going into Europe' is not straightforward and will require a clear strategic plan. Some issues for consideration are:

- Someone (in a senior position) in the business must undertake market research into the proposed EU market(s).
- Marketing policies will need to be adapted. What 'works' in one country will not necessarily work in another for cultural reasons. A distributor must be found (preferably one who is a foreign national), and the terms and conditions attached to sales they make clearly established.
- Businesses will need to ensure that some of their employees are able to communicate in other languages and have an understanding of different cultures.
- Alongside competition for customers, the free movement of labour means that the nature of the pay and conditions offered will affect the firm's ability to attract the best staff.
- Banking facilities to deal with foreign sales must be established. Consideration must be given to the cashflow implications of selling abroad.
- The business will have to ensure that packaging, labelling etc. complies with EU law. This may well mean a complete review of the production process.
- The possibility of the exchange rate changing and 'moving against' the business must be considered (see below).

The euro

In 1999, most of the EU's member countries gave up their individual currencies and adopted the common currency of the euro. The reasoning was straightforward: it made little sense to have a single market with common regulations but with each country having a different currency.

Advantages

The euro has several advantages for businesses:

- Prices are transparent. It is very easy to compare prices of raw material inputs and capital equipment now that all countries have the same currency. It is easier for businesses to keep costs down.
- Trade should be encouraged. Costs are lower because there are no currency exchange charges to pay.
- There is less uncertainty about what will happen to costs and also profits. There is no exchange rate for businesses trading with each other in different countries in the Eurozone. However, for a UK business, a fall in the sterling exchange rate will make imported EU raw materials more expensive. This causes lower profit margins (or may even wipe out any profit) for firms that have to buy such materials. Alternatively, the rate of exchange may rise, making the euro price of exports rise, which will lower demand for UK products.

Disadvantages

There are also disadvantages for businesses:

- There is much greater centralisation of policy making for those members of the euro. This means that the parliaments of individual member states lose some sovereignty over the decisions affecting their businesses.
- All countries in the Eurozone have the same rate of interest, which is set by the European Central Bank. This may not matter if all economies are at the same stage in the economic cycle, but if some are expanding too fast and some are in a recession, what rate should be adopted? Higher rates are necessary to cure the inflation, but the correct policy for a recession is to lower them. Businesses in the countries where the rate that is set is 'wrong' are going to suffer. There will be too much demand or too little.
- A country that joins the euro can no longer devalue its currency to make its exports cheaper (see pp. 43–46). It therefore gives up a major tool of economic policy that could previously have been used to help its businesses become more competitive.

Analysis

You will not be asked to analyse the implications of the UK joining the euro. However, an analysis of the impact on a business of a change in the pound/euro exchange rate could certainly be undertaken — especially if the information in the case study indicates that the business trades (or is planning to start trading) in the EU. Other opportunities for analysis come from considering the implications for a business of a change in an EU law (e.g. on employment or labelling).

Evaluation

This could be demonstrated by judging whether a business should start to trade (or cease trading) with firms in the EU via a consideration of the costs and benefits of this course of action. Alternatively, suggesting the most important factors that would determine the outcome of this decision would be a route into evaluation marks. Another possibility would be justifying the best strategy to deal with a change in the exchange rate (or legislation) in the context of the case study.

Businesses and the law

Laws mean that there are legal minimum standards that must be adhered to by all businesses, and it is essential for a business to keep up with any changes in the law that occur. It is no defence in court for a manager or employee to say that they were not aware of the law.

Important areas of legislation

It is important to know the main pieces of legislation that affect a business's strategic decisions. Three important areas of legislation are described below.

Treatment of employees

- **Contracts of employment.** A contract of employment is an agreement between a business and an employee, under which each of them has certain obligations. The existence of a contract means that both the business and the employee are clear about their rights and responsibilities.
- **Prevention of discrimination.** Discrimination occurs if an employer treats one employee less favourably than another (e.g. when employing or promoting someone) without any justification for doing so. Various Acts exist, such as the Sex Discrimination Act (1975), the Race Relations Act (1976) and the Disability Discrimination Act (1995). Since 2003 there have been similar laws relating to a person's sexual orientation and religion. In October 2006, age discrimination was prohibited under the Employment Equality (Age) Regulations.
- **Minimum wage (1999).** There is a minimum level of pay per hour to which all employees in the UK (except those under 18) are entitled.
- **Health and Safety Act (1974).** This has been developed since 1974 to take account of new safety issues that have emerged. All businesses have 'a duty to take reasonable care' of employees, and furthermore criminal law lays down minimum safety requirements. There is a legal obligation on managers to create a safe and healthy working environment.

Consumer protection

- **Sale of Goods Act (1979).** All goods must be of 'satisfactory quality', must be 'as described' and must be 'fit for the purpose for which they were intended'.
- **Trade Descriptions Act (1968).** The description of the goods on sale must not be false or misleading. This applies to verbal as well as written descriptions.
- **Weights and Measures Act (1985).** It is an offence to 'undersell' a quantity of a product or to give an incorrect indication of the amount of a product on sale.

Relationship between businesses

- **Contract law.** A contract is a legally binding agreement between two or more parties. A contract might, for example, relate to quantity (and quality) of a product to be delivered on a particular date. It is illegal for one party to change the terms of the contract without the other's agreement.
- **Competition law.** In the UK (and, in fact, in the whole of the EU), it is illegal for businesses to restrict competition by joining together to restrict supply or keep prices artificially high.

A strategic approach to complying with the law

It is usual for the government to announce changes in the law well in advance, so that compliance with the change can be built into a business's strategic planning process. The implications are therefore as follows:

- Discussion of any proposals should start at board level as soon as possible. The management of any change in the legislation relating to the firm must start at senior level. Employees cannot simply be expected to know how they are to behave when the law changes.

- The actual detail of the legislation may be complicated, and it may be necessary (and, in the long run, cost effective) to seek specialist legal advice.
- Changes in the law could well affect some of the business's stakeholders — especially employees — and their views on the changes should be sought.

Overall, the business's senior managers need to come up with a policy detailing how the new law will be applied within the business — and also what disciplinary action will occur if an employee does not adhere to the policy.

- Managers should ensure that all employees are aware of this policy and its implications: for example, that it is unlawful for someone to be discriminated against, bullied or harassed on the grounds of gender, race and sexual orientation. Will this communication take place during work time or will some employees have to be paid to attend a training session?
- The policy needs to be reviewed and monitored by managers. The Acts impose a continuing duty on a business to comply.

The discussion, policy formulation and communication to those affected has resource implications for a business in terms of time and money. Introducing new legislation can be costly.

Benefits of compliance with the law

These include the following:
- It avoids bad publicity. Major breaches of the law can make the national news. A poor reputation can deter customers and also potential employees, which, in turn, can affect the level of sales and future growth prospects.
- Fines and compensation payments (which can be large, particularly in matters of health and safety) can be avoided. Both of these damage the business financially.
- Health and safety legislation is an area where employees and managers should, in theory, have a common interest. A good working relationship in accordance with the law in this area may result in better industrial relations in other areas.
- If health and safety is poor and/or the firm does not follow the law in relation to discrimination, employees will be less motivated.
- Applying the laws relating to discrimination should make it more likely that the person with the talents most applicable to the post will be employed, regardless of his or her race, sex or age.
- Going to court to settle a dispute creates a winner and a loser. This is not likely to lead to harmonious industrial relations once the case is concluded.

Analysis

It is certainly important to be able to explain the nature of the various Acts, and there are many others in addition to those above (e.g. on the termination of employment and industrial relations). But the key element in gaining marks for analysis is the ability to suggest the likely implications for the business in the case study of complying (or not complying) with the law.

The development of a strategy (i.e. a series of clear steps for employees at all levels in the firm to follow) for introducing a new law will be evaluative. A judgement on the most significant impact on the business of a new piece of legislation would also access Level 4.

Political issues

Political changes from any country can have implications for UK businesses. The actions of the UK government are likely to be most significant, but UK businesses are also affected by government action in the USA and Europe, particularly as far as demand for goods and services is concerned.

European Union

- The UK is subject to all the rules passed by the EU. These include regulations and directives, such as rules on the maximum size of heavy goods vehicles (HGVs) and on food hygiene.
- The single European market was introduced in 1999. This included legislation on the movement of people, free movement of capital and the removal of internal tariffs.
- The result has been an increase in competition, an increase in the size of the market and an increase in multinational companies like Nestlé.

European Monetary Union

- The EU introduced the single currency, the euro, in 1999. The UK chose not to join the EMU at that point.
- This means that there are transaction costs in changing currency when trade takes place between the UK and an EU country using the euro.
- Some multinational companies may have located outside the UK to gain the advantage of being in the Eurozone.
- Businesses in the financial sector, where there are large daily movements of money, may be seriously disadvantaged.

Effects of EU enlargement

- In recent years the EU has grown rapidly in size, particularly as eastern European countries such as Hungary and the Czech Republic have joined.
- Many of these eastern European countries have a lower standard of living than the earlier members of the EU. In some cases their economies are still very fragile and prone to business failure.
- A number of UK firms have moved their production to the new member states to take advantage of cheaper labour.

- There is a high demand for new infrastructure, such as roads and communications systems, in these countries, creating opportunities for UK firms.
- UK business has also been able to take advantage of the labour coming to the UK from these countries. These workers can often fill skills or supply gaps in the UK labour force. However, at times of higher unemployment their residence may cause problems with UK nationals through competition for scarce employment.
- The management of businesses trading within the EU need to be aware of the many different markets that exist. The gains to be made are often high, but they are accompanied by high risks.

Central government intervention

The extent to which the government will intervene in the economy depends on:
- the political views of the party in power
- the state of the economy — for example, is there a recession or boom in economic activity?
- the views of the electorate on intervention by government on a particular issue
- the wishes of business leaders

Competition policy

In the UK, monopolies are allowed to exist as long as they do not operate against consumers' interests. In the UK, a monopoly is defined as any business controlling 25% or more of the market. The Competition Commission may also investigate proposed mergers and takeovers if their result will be less choice for consumers.

Privatisation and deregulation

- Since the 1980s, a number of public sector utilities have been passed into the private sector. In addition, governments have removed some of the legislation that limited business competition.
- To avoid problems of overpricing after privatisation, a number of regulatory bodies, such as Ofwat and Ofcom, were established. These regulators can limit price increases and demand investment. In 2009, the water companies were set limits for price increases over the following 5 years and given target figures for investment.
- Outdated rules that stifled competition were removed. For example, the ancient laws controlling street markets and the days that they could operate were reviewed and changed.

Labour markets

In recent years, government policy to help keep people in employment has operated on the supply side rather than the demand side, as previously. These measures are designed to try to encourage people into work by giving them the right skills, while removing all the laws and restrictions that might discourage employers from taking on workers. The government has also introduced a range of legislation on equal opportunities and discrimination in the workplace.

Supply-side policies

- Training and education are vital in ensuring that the labour force is skilled and flexible. The government has introduced a number of training initiatives for young people and those who are made redundant.
- Rules controlling part-time working have been removed or revised.
- Trade union legislation has been overhauled since the 1980s, ensuring that it does not restrict the supply of labour.

Minimum wage legislation

- Minimum wage legislation has the benefit of ensuring that workers are paid a reasonable rate for the work that they do.
- For employers, the effect of the minimum wage may be to increase their costs, although many employers choose to pay above the minimum wage.
- There are some employers who still operate outside the law by not paying minimum wage levels. This is most likely to happen where workers are isolated and unaware of the law.

Analysis

To analyse questions involving political issues, it is possible to look at the effects of political actions on the success of businesses. For example, a change in legislation on working hours would have implications for businesses in terms of their costs and their ability to hire extra labour with the required skills. This might also affect the firm's ability to meet demand and reduce its profitability.

Evaluation

To evaluate, it is either necessary to compare the short-term effects of a political action with the long-term effects or to weigh up the pros and cons of a political action. For example, a decision to join the European Monetary System (EMS) might cause problems for a business in the short term, but in the long term it might result in a larger market and improved profits. The business might then have to take the strategic decision to try to achieve growth in European markets.

Social change

Successful businesses need to be aware of changes in the society in which they operate.

Demographic changes

These are changes in the distribution of the population. Any changes will have an impact on the demand that a business faces.

- In recent years, there has been an increase in the proportion of the population in the older age groups because of longer life expectancy. The growth in the 'grey economy' increases the demand for goods and services such as stair lifts and cruises.
- More recently, the birth rate in the UK has started to rise sharply. This will increase the demand for baby products and nursery places.
- The ethnic distribution of the UK is constantly changing. For example, many workers have come to work in the UK since countries like Poland and Hungary joined the EU.

Changing patterns of employment

- **Employment of women.** The majority of women in the UK are in employment today, either full time or part time. This increases the need for childcare and flexible working hours. Businesses have to offer women maternity leave and flexible return conditions by law. Many firms go beyond the legal requirements to ensure that they do not lose female workers.
- **Education.** Most young people now stay in some form of education beyond the age of 16. There has also been a big increase in the number of students going on to higher education. From the business point of view there has been a decline in the number of apprenticeships offered, but an increase in vocational day release courses at colleges.
- **Flexibility.** Businesses today need more flexibility from their employees. This is particularly the case in the retail sector with 24-hour/7-day opening.
- **Technology.** Rapid developments in computerisation, video conferencing, etc. require businesses to invest in training for their employees.
- **Agency work.** The use of agency work has also increased. This gives businesses more flexibility in adapting to changing employment needs. It also means that the business does not need to be concerned with pay as you earn (PAYE) or recruitment.

Corporate responsibility

This is a relatively new area of awareness for firms. Businesses now realise that it is not enough to deliver a good or service to the consumer. They need to be aware of the wider concerns of the public in areas such as ethical behaviour and concern for the environment; they also need to offer good customer service at all times.

- **Environment.** Publicity about environmental concerns has made many businesses concerned to show themselves in a good light, both to their customers and to the media. Hence the recent attempts by supermarkets to reduce the use of plastic carrier bags.
- **Charity and fundraising.** This is a good way for businesses to receive positive publicity in the communities where they operate or with their customers. Examples are companies giving computers or sports equipment to schools.
- **Diversity.** Many businesses now recognise the importance of reflecting the diversity of the population among employees and consumers. Recruitment

policies for new staff have to offer equal opportunities. Goods and services are provided for different groups in society.

- **Financial responsibility.** Since the collapse of some pension funds and the banking crisis of 2008–09, it has been recognised that businesses need to show their employees and customers that they are behaving responsibly in their management of financial affairs.

Analysis

The discussion of social change offers many opportunities for the use of analysis. If a business is facing changes in society, it will need to adapt its strategy accordingly. For example, if a UK business like a private nursery can see that the birth rate is starting to rise, it can adopt a strategy of growth, knowing that there will be a larger potential market at some point in the future and the chance to increase revenue.

Evaluation

Using the example of the nursery school, it is possible to go on to evaluate the way in which the business should react to the social change of an increase in the birth rate. In the short term, the business will need to do market research to find out where competitors operate and also to find those areas where birth rate rises will have most impact. Some areas will not be affected because they have a large proportion of elderly people.

In the long term, having identified the best markets, the nursery business can then start its growth and expansion plans by opening new nurseries.

Technological change

Technology changes at an increasingly rapid rate; it is important that businesses keep up with these changes if they are going to be able to compete effectively.

Effects of technology on business

- New technology is often associated in the minds of employees with unemployment. It is therefore perceived as a threat. This makes the introduction of new technology difficult for managers and employees.
- New technology usually involves new skills and the need for training, imposing costs on the business and stress on employees.
- New technology will always involve change of some sort. Most people find change in the workplace difficult to cope with. At its worst, the situation can leave workers feeling displaced and unwanted, resulting in a fall in motivation and efficiency.
- In some countries, such as Japan, change is welcomed and regarded as exciting and desirable. This is seldom the case in the UK.

Benefits of technological change

- New technology can bring a net increase in employment if it results in an increase in demand. The use of call centres has resulted in a rise in employment opportunities in this sector.
- Firms that introduce new technology are often vibrant and encouraging places to work, and they will, therefore, often find it easier to recruit the best workers.
- For employees, learning new skills can improve morale and self-esteem, resulting in better motivation and productivity.
- Managers and employees need to realise that continuing to do the same thing carries the highest risks of all.

Implementing technological change

- One important factor is getting the timing right. Holding back for too long on introducing new technology might result in competitors taking market share. Starting too soon might mean that the technology is insufficiently tried and tested.
- It is important to look at the use of new technology as it will fit into the overall business situation. A strategic decision is vitally important.
- Sometimes it may be better not to buy the new technology but to outsource instead. This is particularly true when changes in technology are very rapid.
- It is important not to assume that new technology will always give better results. Research into both the uses of the capital investment and the potential market is always vitally important before large amounts are spent on investment.

Analysis

Analysis can be done in the context of the effects for the business of investing in technology. For example, it would be possible to discuss the long-term impact on a business's success and profitability if there was insufficient investment in new technology at a time when competitors were moving forward. It is also possible to analyse the effects of new technology on the motivation of the workforce and its implications for productivity and output.

Evaluation

Evaluation can be achieved by considering where the business wants to be in the long term and what strategic changes this will require in terms of new technology and employment. If a business decides to invest in new technology, such as the computerisation of an assembly line, this will require effective long-term strategic planning. There will need to be reorganisation of the work area, training of staff and new methods of quality control. To make all this work, managers will have to plan carefully and hold discussions with those concerned in the changes at every point. It is also possible to discuss the most significant implications for a business resulting from the introduction of new technology.

The environment

The environment is a highly topical and emotive topic which is now of importance to all businesses.

External factors

Damaging the environment is often described as imposing:
- an external cost
- a negative externality

It is important that you are able to recognise both of the above terms, although they refer to the same thing!

They refer to costs that are incurred by others and not the actual user. Driving a car means that the owner will have private costs to pay to use the car, namely the cost of the petrol. However, the community incurs costs in terms of pollution (noise and air), congestion and the cost of health treatments as a result of carbon emissions.

A global issue

China uses coal as a major source of power, and consequently causes a significant amount of damage to the environment. Cars and plane journeys and an inefficient use of fuel also contribute negatively to our environment through carbon emissions. To what extent is open to debate.

Persuading people to use alternative forms of transport is not easy, as the convenience of the car and the desire to travel are significant attractions. New electric cars are being developed, but they still require an initial source of energy, which creates emissions.

Various conferences and high-level meetings have been held around the world in order to attempt to tackle emissions and the like. Unfortunately, from Kyoto to more recent conferences, agreements have been minimal.

Consequences of pollution

Air pollution
Beijing in China and Athens in Greece are classic examples of how poor air quality can quickly create 'smog', which in turn can affect the health of the population, and thus create costs for the health services of those countries. This money spent on dealing with the health issues caused by pollution could have been spent on other areas in the economies of these countries.

Sea/water pollution
Oil spillages are frequent occurrences, although serious disasters are thankfully less frequent. Nevertheless, such spillages are harmful to wildlife and the fishing

industry, and can damage tourism as the oil comes ashore. In addition, there is the cost of clearing up the oil, which has to be paid by someone. Water supplies can be damaged, as the oil can filter into river systems. Chemicals and other industrial discharges harm our rivers, increasing the cost of providing clean water to drink.

Land pollution

Mining, quarrying and deforestation affect the ability of the land to provide continuous resources. Many of the world's resources are finite, and once used sustainability is negatively affected. Deforestation in South America has taken place in order to satisfy the world's demand for wood and to provide agricultural land for its inhabitants. Unfortunately, much of the land is now parched and unable to sustain agricultural produce.

Noise pollution

Houses near to motorways and major roads suffer not only from air pollution but also from the incessant noise of the traffic. Similarly, houses under the flight paths of planes, close to airports, also suffer from intense noise. Some factories can also be noisy, affecting the lives of nearby residents.

Sight pollution

In an attempt to lessen the amount of air pollution, the usage of wind turbines has increased significantly. However, there are people who protest about the placement of such methods of generating power due to their size and appearance. Placing more wind turbines out to sea has also met with objections on the grounds of spoiling the view.

Overall consequences

The main consequences appear to be the effects that pollution has had, or is having, on the world's climate. Recent examples of extreme weather conditions have heightened the debate about the consequences of pollution. Scientists appear not to be able to agree on what is actually happening. Nevertheless, governments around the world are passing legislation in order to reduce the amount of pollution, or at least extract an additional cost to business and consumers for contributing to it.

Businesses need to be mindful about their levels of polluting and the additional costs that may be incurred. Such matters affect the ability of a business to achieve its objectives, as pollution legislation and monetary factors impinge upon the business as constraints.

Government measures

Sustainable Development Strategy

This is a package of measures aimed at reducing emission levels within the country:

- incentives for purchasing low-emission cars (lower excise duty)
- landfill tax increases to encourage the reduction of waste generation
- increased tax allowances for businesses that invest in environmentally friendly technology

- additional recycling schemes
- moving freight off roads and on to rail (sponsored by the EU Transport Committee) — incentives to utilise rail rather than road
- environmental stewardship — finance for farmers for effective environmental usage of their land
- waste management programme aimed at reducing the amount of biodegradable waste — targets set to reduce such waste to 50% of 1995 levels by 2013
- climate change levy — a tax paid by industry on the usage of energy
- Carbon Trust Standard — launched in 2008 as a kitemark for being environmentally friendly
- car adverts — to include carbon emissions and fuel consumption
- congestion charges — introduced in London, firstly at £5, now £8 per car, in an attempt to discourage car usage in the centre of London
- scrappage scheme for cars — grant of £2,000 to trade in cars over 10 years old for new, more fuel-efficient cars with reduced emissions (ended in 2010)
- home insulation grants — to save energy when heating homes
- alternative energy sources — an increased number of wind farms and tidal energy
- Kyoto Treaty (1997) — committing nations to reduce greenhouse gases by 5% within 10 years.

Analysis

Analysis marks can be gained by offering comments about how the business in the case will be affected either by environmental issues or by any government initiatives to improve the environment. Being mindful of how the various stakeholders of the business will react or be affected by the business is also an obvious route into Level 3 marks.

Many of the implications may be related to costs. However, rather than just stating the obvious fact that costs may rise, it is much better to elaborate by suggesting which costs will rise and therefore the consequences for the business of such increases in costs. Will the increase in costs affect the profitability of the business, or its ability to achieve its objectives? Can the business afford to pass on the increased costs to its consumers? Are there other factors within the case that mean such increases in costs will compound an existing problem?

In other words, be prepared to elaborate sufficiently to gain the Level 3 marks.

Evaluation

To gain marks for evaluation, it is necessary to offer a judgement which is justified in the context of the case and the question. Offering a judgement as to the most likely consequence or which factor will affect the business the most is an acceptable route into Level 4 marks. Good evaluation will involve weighing the evidence in a balanced manner (thinking about the positive and negative consequences) before selecting the most likely outcome. It is always a good strategy to consider the evidence in the light of the business's objectives.

The management of change

Any process of change will require strategic decision making. Questions on this module will almost always be about the need for a firm to make changes, or about a decision to change long-term objectives forcing change on to management. Most people find change unsettling and worrying. If it is not handled well, it can lead to problems of industrial unrest and demotivation.

The long-running postal dispute of 2009 showed how difficult it was for the managers to introduce change. Workers are suspicious of management aims, and managers may feel that workers are always resistant to more efficient working practices. For change to occur smoothly, open and frank communication between managers and workers is essential at every step. If either party feels that there are things happening behind the scenes, this will affect the outcome, and confidence and trust will disappear.

The causes of change

Internal change

Internal change may result from the following factors:

- **Objectives.** As a business grows, its objectives may change from survival to profitability, or from profitability to growth (see p. 15). Each change will require a different emphasis for the firm. For example, a new business will need to keep a very careful eye on cashflow.
- **Personnel.** Changes in management will have an effect on the way a business is run. A new chief executive will bring different ideas and ways of doing things that will have an impact on the whole business.
- **Skill levels.** Changes in the skill levels of employees and the availability of skilled labour will have an effect on the management of change in the business. If a business finds it difficult to recruit suitable workers, this will have an impact on the day-to-day management of production.
- **Finances.** The ease with which a business can raise finance will also affect the management of change. Lack of finance will create difficulties and may often prevent a business from growing as rapidly as it would wish.
- **Innovation.** In some markets, the requirement for innovation and to be at the forefront of new ideas is of paramount importance. Managing the rapid changes that this requires is difficult, but for those who do it successfully, the possible rewards can be very high.

External change

External change may result from the following factors:

- **Globalisation.** The growth of China and India as important industrial nations has had huge implications for world trade. Businesses in the UK have had to adapt to these emerging nations by taking account of the markets they offer for British goods. They also present a competitive threat through their lower-wage economies. Improved communications mean that service sector businesses, such as call centres, can now locate easily in a country like India.

- **The environment.** Many firms have had to adapt their organisation and what they produce to take account of environmental factors. The car industry has realised the need to produce energy-efficient and low-emission cars to meet public demand.
- **Technology.** The speed of technological change demands that firms adapt and change, or face losing markets to those firms which are more adaptable.
- **The customer base.** Changes in the distribution of the UK population, whether by age or ethnic group, mean that businesses need to adapt to the changing demands of their consumers. For example, immigration from eastern Europe has required supermarkets in some areas to offer different ranges of food.
- **The economy.** Businesses have always needed to change the scale of their operation according to the state of the domestic and international economy. Production will need to be scaled back at times of recession and increased when the economy booms.
- **Competition.** It is vital that a business is aware of its competition and that it takes measures to secure or increase its market share. Businesses such as Aldi and Lidl have forced the larger supermarkets to offer lower-priced goods in order to retain customers affected by the credit crunch.
- **The government.** Legislation will force change on to a business. The introduction of minimum wage legislation meant that all firms needed to consider how much they were paying their lower-skilled and younger workers. Laws on food labelling have affected food processors and supermarkets.

The management of change

- This is likely to be one of the most difficult tasks for managers. The best managers deal with change effectively; others handle it badly. Those managers who handle it badly do so either by ignoring the need for change or by introducing it without consultation in a rushed and ill-considered manner.
- Anticipated change is often the result of good forecasting or market research. It allows managers to think through change and discuss it openly with those concerned.
- Unanticipated change is, by its nature, much more difficult to deal with. The most effective businesses have plans in place to help them cope with situations like 9/11 or the winter of 2009–10. The effects may still be extensive, but a contingency plan will help a firm deal with the problems and work through them.

Factors for managing change successfully

In order to manage change successfully, it is necessary to take account of the following factors:

- There needs to be an atmosphere of trust between managers and workers.
- Communication is vital.
- Businesses cannot afford to be static for too long in modern economies. If workers are used to change and see the results of it, they will be much more likely to accept change in the future.

- Employees must be included in the process of change so that they feel a sense of 'ownership'.
- Managers need to be prepared to listen to employees' ideas. They may not always accept them, but it is important that employees feel they have a part to play.
- Management needs to have a clear strategic plan for the process of change.

Changing location

The strategic decision to move to a new location can be very difficult to manage. The reasons for deciding to move might be:

- a lower-cost location
- the availability of cheaper labour
- the availability of suitably qualified labour
- limits on expansion at the current site
- the personal wishes of the owner
- a larger consumer base

The decision to relocate is one which needs careful consideration. It is a situation that is likely to worry current workers, who may not want or be able to move to a different site. In making this strategic decision, managers need to consider carefully how effectively the business will be able to operate in the location. The decision may result in a more efficient business, but it could also be a costly mistake.

Analysis

It will be possible to gain analysis marks by discussing the implications of any change for the business. For example, if management decides that it is going to relocate a business to a new site in eastern Europe, there will be a number of implications. Management will need to consider the availability of trained labour at the new site. It will also have to take account of the cost of making workers redundant in the UK. Although the costs may be lower at the new site, there will considerable costs incurred in making the move.

Evaluation

The discussion about the business relocating to eastern Europe could look at the short- and long-term implications. In the short term, the business would have increased costs from redundancies and starting up at the new site. In the long term, it may gain from lower labour costs, a more flexible workforce and proximity to its main markets. As a result, the strategic objectives of the business may change.

Change within the business

It is important for businesses to be willing to accept change and to discuss it openly with all those involved (stakeholders). Creating the right environment for change to work is not always easy.

Leadership and motivation effects

Leadership and motivation can have important effects on the management of change:

- **Teamwork.** The role of teamwork in the workplace has increased in recent years. Making workers responsible for tasks encourages pride in the job and increases motivation.
- **Cooperation.** Enlightened managers understand that a motivated workforce is an efficient one. To use motivation effectively, managers need to engender a spirit of trust in the workplace.
- **Organisational culture.** Creating an atmosphere of trust and cooperation does not mean that change will be easy, but it does mean that there will be an ethos that makes workers willing to listen and be flexible.

Role of employer/employee relations

Individual relations

The more distant workers are from their managers, the more likely it is that problems will occur. Management needs to know about workers' conditions and jobs and to understand their concerns. Mutual understanding is essential.

Collective relations — trade unions

- The role of the trade unions and industrial relations legislation is covered on pp. 65–67.
- Trade unions exist to protect the rights of their members. This often puts them into conflict with managers.
- On occasions, a more sympathetic management approach might help avert industrial action.
- In recent years, Japanese work practices and single union agreements have been used by UK firms.
- Other schemes have been used elsewhere. These include no-strike deals, pendulum arbitration and the use of the Advisory, Conciliation and Arbitration Service (ACAS) to mediate in disputes.

New working practices

Changes in the retail sector and in the role of women in the workforce have resulted in a number of changes in working practices. These include:

- flexible hours (flexitime) requiring a designated number of hours, some of which must cover the core or busiest time of the day
- job sharing
- a rapid increase in part-time work, mainly as a result of 24-hour, 7-day trading by retailers
- home working using modern technology

Analysis

As in the previous section, it is possible to achieve analysis marks by looking at the effects of introducing changes. The introduction of job sharing may help a business keep its female members of staff, particularly those with babies and young children, but there will be costs involved in operating it.

Evaluation

It is possible to evaluate by looking at the short- and long-term effects of making changes in a business. The introduction of flexible working might be costly in the short run, but in the long run it might mean that the business does not have to recruit and train new workers to replace those who cannot manage to work full time.

Industrial relations and change

The ability to manage change effectively can give a business a competitive advantage in a dynamic environment. 'Macho management' can certainly be used to impose change, but this is likely to bring resentment. Change will be easier where managers and employees work together and are willing to compromise and cooperate. Positive industrial relations (the relationship between management and employees) are a significant factor that will help facilitate this.

The beneficial effects of employees being consulted and participating in decisions runs through much of modern management theory and can help with the management of change in several ways:

- Participation should mean better communication between managers and employees.
- Employees will feel that 'their view counts' and they may become more motivated and productive because of the consultation.
- Managers can never 'know it all' and may in fact be ill-informed about the realities of the workplace.
- Consultation is a legal requirement on issues such as redundancy, health and safety, and changes to contracts of employment.

Recognising a union

Consultation is often conducted via a trade union. When a union is 'recognised' by an employer, its existence is accepted and the managers agree to negotiate with it over terms and conditions of employment. This negotiation is known as **collective bargaining**. Union recognition demonstrates a readiness to treat employees as stakeholders. There are a number of benefits to this that can help improve motivation and productivity:

- There will be better communication between managers and employees. This can help to highlight difficulties before they develop into a serious industrial relations problem.
- It will help managers to identify employees' training needs.
- It will help managers to comply with health and safety procedures.

However:

- It could be argued that recognition will restrict 'a manager's right to manage'.
- Union representatives will ask for better wages and conditions as a matter of course and will probably do so when change is being negotiated as well.

The management of change

A union may well be involved, but even if a union is not involved, if a firm is serious about employee consultation in the process of managing change there are certain issues to resolve:

- When will the meetings be held? Employees may not want to attend a meeting before or after work unless they are paid. There are cost implications here.
- How many employees will be involved? Will employees be drawn from all areas of the business? A larger group is more representative but meetings will be harder to manage. How will they be chosen? Will employees vote for representatives or will managers ask for volunteers?
- Who will 'cover' for the employees while they are being consulted? Also, what if the business operates a bonus scheme and/or employees are on some sort of piecework scheme? How will payments be affected by 'absence' due to the consultation?

However, just because a process exists where employees and managers can meet and talk does not mean that all parties are content and that successful change is always achieved. It will depend to a large extent on:

- whether employees' views are actually listened to and considered carefully, and at least some of their points are accepted
- whether employees accept that their views are not automatically going to be accepted and acted upon
- whether either side treats the meetings as an opportunity to 'badmouth' the other
- whether employees accept that they are going to be involved in decisions that might be difficult for them (e.g. redundancy)

The costs of consultation

Consultation incurs the following costs:

- There are costs in terms of managers' and employees' time.
- There are financial costs, as employees have the right to be paid during a consultation process if it takes place in work time.
- Decision making is definitely going to be slower with employee participation — especially if the firm is taking the process seriously. Any consultation period will have to be built into the process of strategic planning.

In spite of these it is to be hoped that better decisions, i.e. ones which have support from all parties, will be made.

ACAS and the process of change

One very important way in which industrial relations can be improved and change successfully achieved is through employees and managers following ACAS guidelines. ACAS stands for Advisory, Conciliation and Arbitration Service.

ACAS is a government-funded, but completely independent, industrial relations service. Its role is to:
- give advice on industrial relations to employees and managers— ACAS guidelines exist on every aspect of employment and workplace procedure
- offer a service of conciliation, trying to reconcile two different positions and get each party to see the other's view
- provide arbitration (if both parties agree) — an ACAS assessor will decide between two conflicting claims.

ACAS is widely respected. Employment tribunals often refer to ACAS when making a judgement. It can be helpful whatever the nature of the employee consultation. It does not matter whether it is a one-off consultation about an initiative such as the introduction of flexitime or a no-strike deal, or whether an ongoing system of consultation is going to be developed. In either event, ACAS can provide the guidelines to help make the process work. Advice is also available on any aspect of industrial relations. If managers want to avoid a dispute and achieve successful change, they should try to abide by these guidelines. The same applies to employees.

Analysis

It will be essential to consider the likely impact of any proposed change on the stake-holders of the business. In doing this you will be analysing the reasons why these groups (particularly the employees) may be resistant to it.

Evaluation

The development of a strategy (i.e. a series of clear steps for managers to follow) for introducing the change would be evaluative. Such a strategy would include the extent and nature of the consultation process with the business's employees. A judgement on which stakeholder(s) will be the most significantly affected by the change would also access Level 4.

This section comprises a case study for you to look at and answer. It is a full F297 paper which is very similar in case content and the amount and type of questions to the paper you will get when you sit the actual exam.

The mark allocation and format mirrors what you will be faced with in your actual module examination. However, for question 1, we have included *two* examples for question 1(a). It is important for you realise that this is only to give you a taste of the possible areas to be examined.

It is strongly recommended that you attempt the questions before you read the candidates' answers. This will allow you to compare answers and at the same time encourage you to practise your exam technique.

It is important to make it really clear how you have attempted any numerate question, stating any formulae used and clearly setting the work out to make it easier for an examiner to follow. Just because there is now a numerate question, this does **not** mean that there will not be other opportunities for you to use numbers; on the contrary, this is to be encouraged as the case will always contain vital numerate information. Good candidates will use the numerate information in other questions, where appropriate.

Once you have attempted the case study questions, it is recommended that you look at the initial examiner's commentary, which highlights the type of answer that is expected.

Following this are the answers written by examination candidates. Included within their answers are letters (A), (B) etc, which correspond to the examiner's comments that follow each answer. A real attempt has been made to show you exactly what is rewarded and what is not. The comments also clearly highlight within the candidates' answers where a particular level of response is gained. At the end of each answer and following the examiner's comments, the mark awarded for the question is shown. Finally, the total mark and grade awarded are shown.

At the end of the guide, a detailed mark scheme is provided as an appendix to show you how marks are allocated for each question and level. It is important to notice the range of marks that can be awarded for the different levels of response. This shows that it is essential to offer analysis and evaluation if you hope to achieve the highest marks. It may be useful to use the mark scheme as you read through the candidates' answers.

Case study: Learning for Life Ltd

Learning for Life (LFL) was started by Tamara and Chris Parry in 2000. The business operates from offices based in Taunton, Somerset. They started by selling academic magazines to schools and colleges which wanted up-to-date information and examples that could be used by students to enhance their understanding of, initially, business studies and economics. The business quickly expanded and now sells magazines for a wide range of subjects. LFL employs six staff who are responsible for ensuring material is produced on time and for setting up the layout of the magazines and press releases. There are two other staff who market the material to the educational establishments.

Chris had realised that textbooks go out-of-date very quickly and that a regular monthly issue of a magazine would help to solve the problem of keeping abreast of the latest events.

Publishing academic material is highly competitive and, as a consequence, anything different has tended to be popular with both students and teachers alike.

Tamara and Chris have set themselves a target of retiring before they are 50 years old. Now with only 12 years before they reach that age, Tamara is keen to ensure profits continue to grow — if possible, at an even faster rate.

Chris, who is the 'ideas man', has managed to expand the portfolio of publications, which now includes not only magazines but also regular press releases that are posted on LFL's websites for a download fee. The press releases relate to specific topics and have data and questions for students to answer. These releases have proved very popular with teachers and also lecturers, who have insufficient time to research such material.

Chris is also working on several additional ideas, including the possibility of producing software that could be sold and used in e-books. The market for e-books and software has grown significantly in a very short time — something that Chris is only too aware of. He wants to be involved and has already had conversations with Zambezee, a distributor of e-books.

Zambezee has shown considerable interest in Chris's ideas for academic material that could be produced to be compatible with e-book hardware. Almost immediately, Zambezee offered LFL a 4-year contract to produce material for several A-level, GCSE and undergraduate markets. Having a contract for 4 years would provide some certainty to the business and Chris could be comfortable in the knowledge that he was dealing with a reputable business that had a significant share of the market.

Both Chris and Zambezee are aware that the markets for up-to-date material are growing rapidly, especially in universities, where the needs of students could be met without their needing to buy expensive textbooks that very quickly become outdated. Tamara is slightly less enthusiastic than Chris, as she does not want the business tied to one company for as long as 4 years, especially in this market. However, she is quite keen to explore the financial implications of Chris's other idea, which would involve leasing out the hardware to schools and then offering a range of software packages. Although this second investment opportunity would require a substantial amount of initial capital outlay, leasing out the hardware to customers would tie them to LFL because the software would be compatible only with the leased hardware.

Leasing the hardware would ensure that potential customers could afford to sign up to LFL, as they would not have the high cost of purchasing the hardware. Chris had even thought of having various packages with differing contract lengths, offering large discounts for the longer contracts.

Tamara, who is responsible for the financial affairs of the business, is constantly looking to reinvest the profits of the business, which have grown substantially over recent years. She looked at Chris's ideas in more detail and showed Chris her results (see Figure 1).

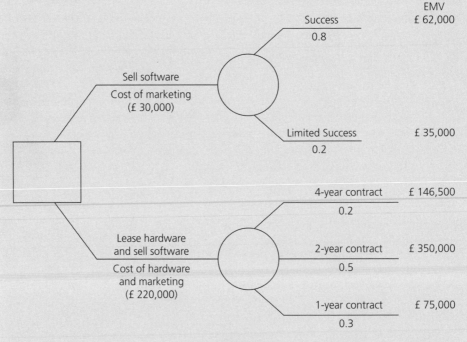

Figure 1

Chris is not convinced, suggesting that there is too much 'guesswork' involved. Nevertheless, they both agreed that one of the ideas is worthy of being adopted.

Whichever scheme is selected, it is obvious that LFL will need to borrow money from the bank in order to cover the cost of setting up and marketing the chosen option. Tamara has already suggested this would not be an issue, given the level of profits LFL is generating on its magazines and what she described as 'a healthy balance sheet' (Appendices 1 and 2).

In addition to Tamara's diagram (Figure 1), LFL has been given figures from an accountant who had produced an initial estimate of the likely net inflows for the two schemes (Table 1). This was based on some of the information Zambezee had given to Chris in the form of sales projections.

Table 1 Estimated net cash inflows for each option (£)

	E-books software only	E-books software and hardware
Initial investment	(30,000)	(220,000)
End of year 1	8,500	69,500
End of year 2	15,500	105,500
End of year 3	18,000	180,000
End of year 4	20,000	195,000

The economic climate is, however, of concern. Although an end to the recession is now in sight, the government has already announced substantial cutbacks to university funding. The government is also attempting to reduce the huge budget deficit that has built up in the last 10 years. Public sector expenditure is being cut across all departments except the health service. Also of concern to LFL are the possible increases in interest rates that might be introduced to help control inflation if it starts to escalate.

It is not all bad news, however: with unemployment rising, last year was a record year for university applications. University was seen as an alternative to claiming the job seeker's allowance!

Another concern is the reported change in copyright laws. At present, authors are protected by copyright. However, publishing software and internet resources are less easy to control and their royalties less easy to attribute. The organisations that exist to ensure authors are paid sufficient royalties for their work have of late been attempting to introduce their own systems to guarantee that authors receive the right amount of royalty payments; the suggested changes in the law will make this harder to achieve.

Table 2 Market segmentation for LFL's customers in previous year

Educational institution	% of magazine sales	% of press release material
Schools	45	25
Colleges	35	30
Universities	20	45

Appendix 1: Balance sheet, as at end of last financial year — unaudited (£s)

Fixed assets	240,000	
Depreciation @10%	24,000	216,000
Current assets		
Stock	22,500	
Debtors	35,000	
Cash	3,450	
Current liabilities		
Creditors	29,700	
Net current assets		31,250
Long-term liabilities		100,000
Net assets		147,250
Initial investment		
(Chris and Tamara)	5,000	
Retained profits		
(prior to last financial year)	142,250	
		147,250

Appendix 2: P&L account for LFL Ltd, year ending last financial year (£s)

Sales revenue	670,000
Cost of sales	250,000
Gross profit	420,000
Less expenses	185,000
Operating profit	235,000
Less interest payable	39,000
Profit before tax	196,000
Less tax	52,000
Profit after tax	144,000
Less dividends	0
Retained profit	144,000

Questions

Answer all the questions:

(1) (a) Using Table **1**, calculate the payback and annual average rate of return (accounting rate of return — ARR) for both options. (13 marks)

OR

    (a) Using Figure **1**, complete the decision tree to find the expected values for each option. (13 marks)

(1) (b) Recommend which option LFL should undertake. Justify your view.
(18 marks)

(2) Evaluate how changes in legislation may impact on the ability of LFL to achieve its objectives. (18 marks)

(3) Evaluate the extent to which competition will affect LFL. (18 marks)

(4) Discuss how a change in the economic climate might affect the success of LFL.
(23 marks)

■ ■ ■

Initial examiner commentary

This paper is essentially about the management of change within the business and the strategies that management uses to deal with the effects of change in the long term. Your focus should be on where the business is now, where it wants to be in the future and how it can achieve that situation through its actions.

Remember that all the questions apply to the case study and that all your answers need to be in context. You can use theory to explain your arguments, but an answer that is purely theoretical will not be likely to achieve above Level 2 marks.

The use of numerical information taken from the case study to back up your arguments (e.g. ratio analysis) will usually achieve Level 3 marks. It is possible to achieve Levels 3 and 4 without using figures, but it will be much more difficult to get to the higher levels.

Most of the questions on this paper require evaluation of the information. The trigger words here are 'discuss', 'evaluate' and 'the extent to which'. The only alternative question on this paper is one that asks for analysis. Answers that are descriptive will be poorly rewarded. You need to remember the ways in which you can achieve evaluation and use them. Look at again at the advice given at the beginning of this book.

(1) (a) This question requires analysis of the decision tree. Try to show as much working as possible, as clearly as you can. Do not simply provide payback and ARR figures or put your numbers on to the decision tree. If your answer is incorrect, but some of your calculations are right, you will still be able to pick up marks. An incorrect answer and no working will earn nothing.

(1) (b), (2), (3) and **(4)** All the other questions on this paper require evaluation. If the question asks for a recommendation or decision on policy, then you should give one and explain the reasons for your decision. In arriving at that point, you should have analysed a number of different situations, using the information that you have been given. It is important that your answer should not be a list. You should aim to analyse two or three points in depth. Explanation of any number of points — however good — will only achieve Level 2 marks.

(1) (b) You need to consider the reliability of the information that you have analysed and Tamara and Chris's attitude to risk taking. How likely is it that Tamara and Chris will be able to raise the finance for this undertaking? What are the opportunity costs of proceeding? How does the product fit with the existing portfolio? Which alternative is more likely to help them reach their objectives?

(2) You need to consider one or two changes in legislation that might affect this business and its future strategy. This could be minimum wage legislation, data protection, health and safety, taxation laws or anything else that you might consider relevant. You should then consider the implications of this for the business. How will the legislation affect the strategies for the future; will there be an impact on growth; might they need to diversify as a consequence?

(3) The first thing to consider here is who the business's competitors are. How contestable is the market? Does the business have a unique selling point? On the other hand, new competition might have no effect on the business, especially if Tamara and Chris have a strategic plan to cope with changes. You should analyse some of these points and then come to a conclusion that you have justified.

(4) For this question you can analyse any economic factor that might affect LFL. This could be monetary or fiscal policy, interest rates, exchange rates or the economic cycle. You need to consider the severity of the factor and the length of time it will affect LFL's business. How income elastic are its products and how likely is the business to achieve its objectives if the economic environment worsens?

■ ■ ■

Answer to case study: candidate A

(1) (a) ARR/payback option

ARR

For software:

Cash in total £62,000

Investment cost £30,000

Profit £32,000

32/4 = 8

8/30

26.7%

ARR is 27%[A]

For software and hardware:

Cash in total £550,000

Investment cost £220,000

Profit £330,000

330/4 = 82.5

82.5/220

ARR is 37.5%

Payback

For software:

The initial cost of £30,000 is covered by inflows between 2 and 3 years. (By the end of year 3, inflows are £42,000. So payback is between 2 and 3 years.)

For software and hardware:

The initial cost of £220,000 is covered by inflows between 2 and 3 years as well. (By the end of year 3 inflows are £350,000.) Payback is the same.[B]

    (A) The working is shown, which is good. The candidate has rounded up, which is acceptable.

    (B) The ARR of both options is correct and the working shown. Analysis is demonstrated. The payback technique is correct but is a pity that the 'final step' in terms of precisely when in the second year the payback for each will occur has not been taken. Full marks were therefore missed.
11/13 marks

(1) (b) Looking at the payback and ARR of each option, it would suggest that leasing out the hardware would be a better strategic decision for LFL. This is because it pays back in 2 years and 3 months, which is 1 month less than Chris's other option. The ARR is 37.5%, which is also better than the other option of selling the software only (ARR for that is 27%), which suggests a higher level of return will occur if the leasing option is chosen compared to the other investment.[A]

However, having said both of these things, the payback difference is just 1 month, showing that there is not much difference between the two options in this respect. Also, the ARR is distorted by the high start-up cost of option 2, which would suggest that either option could be beneficial to LFL. It is also important to recognise that for both of these options the net cash flows are only estimated by the accountant. Furthermore it says that 'this was based on some of the information Zambezee had given to Chris'. It could be the case that Zambezee put their own 'spin' on the figures.**B** So Table 1 is useful in making a decision but Chris and Tamara need to recognise the cash flows are not guaranteed.

The decision tree is more data to consider. It shows LFL should choose the sell software option. This is because the overall outcome of that decision would gain LFL £26,600 as opposed to £6,800 from the leasing.**C** However again, the decision tree is only an estimate and is only as reliable as the figures in it.

The start-up costs of the lease hardware include £220,000 in marketing, whereas the first option only requires £30,000. This is a big issue for LFL as they may find it hard to raise the required amount, due to the fact they are highly geared at 63.59% showing they are mainly financed by loan capital (currently with the £100,000 long-term liabilities). As well as this they have a relatively poor acid test ratio of 1.29 to 1, showing they are not very liquid, which means banks are very unlikely to finance them,**D** especially a sum as large as £220,000 on top of the existing loan of £100,000.

Thirdly the probability of success is a lot higher in the sell software plan at 0.8, meaning they are a lot more likely to reap the rewards, which will help them grow at a faster rate and have more chance of retiring before the age of 50, which are their two objectives.

It is therefore clear to see that option 1 is a better option. Although the ARR and payback of option 2 would suggest it is a better option, these figures are estimates and LFL are unlikely to be able to raise the necessary finance given their gearing and liquidity position. Even if they did raise the money this is a big risk that could threaten the whole business. They may not go bankrupt but it could certainly 'shhot down' their objectives. In the long term there is less of a risk to the business if option 1 is chosen. It is a better strategic decision.**E** The payback figure is only slightly less and the expected value is higher than option 2 anyway, proving that LFL should choose option 1. They are much more likely to gain the finance for it and will give them a much better chance to reach their objectives.

(A) Although the candidate dives straight in with little scene setting, this is no bad thing. The figures are correct and it is good to see quantitative data being used early in the answer.

(B) This is a very good point. Note that instead of simply saying something like 'figures can't always be trusted', reference is made to the case where Zambezee gave the data to Chris, who then gave it to the accountant. The candidate has realised that the data may be suspect. A judgement on the validity of the data is always useful.

(C) Data are there to be used and the information in the decision tree has been.

(D) This is very good analysis involving two simple calculations. All too often candidates are scared of figures, but these calculations should be well within the ability of a candidate at A2.

(E) The last paragraph is an effective summary of the previous analysis and is not just repeating the same sort of point in the same manner. In addition, clear reference is made to the likelihood of gaining the necessary resources for each option, and a link is made to the owners' objectives. Presumably 'shhot down' is meant to be 'shoot down'. The phrase is put in inverted commas, but slang like this should be avoided. The reference to 'a strategic decision' is a bit throwaway, but the phrase 'long term' was also used. This is certainly sufficient for Level 4. A supported decision using quantitative data is made. **15/18 marks**

(2) The objectives of LFL are to grow fast and for Chris and Tamara to retire at 50.

The perspective changes in copyright law could have a significant effect on LFL's ability to achieve its objectives. This is because LFL's press releases are sold online for a download fee. Therefore if the changes to copyright law do take place that increases the risk that somebody could purchase the press releases and pass them on over the internet for no charge, thus depriving LFL of possible customers and profits. If this development was not calculated into the figures when objectives were created, then if copyright laws do come into place the objective will be invalid.**A** This could have a major impact on Tamara and Chris's objective to 'ensure profits continue to grow'. And considering the fact that much of LFL's income is from press releases, this could dent their hopes of expansion.

In general terms LFL will have to take into account that any change to legislation is likely to bring extra costs in order to implement the changes properly. Tamara and Chris would be wise to keep this in mind because although they are looking to achieve their objectives, which involve increasing profits, they may have to keep back some capital rather than reinvesting it. This would enable LFL to be safe if changes to legislation did occur. However, keeping back capital will affect their ability to increase profits, so Tamara and Chris will have to make a decision on the amount of risk they are willing to take in order to achieve their objectives.

Consider a change in the national minimum wage. This is likely to have an effect on LFL as costs are likely to rise as a result. Even if they do not employ staff that are working on the minimum wage, this rise is likely to lead to an overall rise in pay for all employees at any firm as employees will wish to keep the differential between their pay and the minimum wage the same distance apart.**B** If the firm's costs increase and they are unable to balance this rise in costs through another means, it is likely to mean that their profit will decrease. One of their objectives states Tamara wants profit to continue to grow and if possible at an even faster rate. As I suggested before, unless they can raise the price of their products without damaging demand or substantially lower the other costs at the business to counter the rise in wages without affecting the quality of service/product that is sold, this objective does not look to be a viable case.**C**

Another aspect of legislation affecting LFL is the fact that the firm is a private limited company. Being a private company means that it may find it difficult to raise capital for expansion in the future; it cannot float on the stock market. However we have to ask the question is this ever likely? It may be a very long time before they need to take this step. Tamara and Chris may have retired before that point and sold their shares.**D**

In my opinion the most important piece of law is that relating to copyright. If this change actually happens and authors do not get paid what they deserve then they will not write for LFL again. Also they will tell others about it which will limit the whole 'lifeblood' of the business. Also they may sue LFL and if that happens it will be disastrous publicity and possibly a financial loss if LFL lose, both of which would impact severely on the firm's future operations. That is why this law is the most important one.**E** Authors and finance are key resources to LFL's success and if they break the law then fewer authors and less money would be a severe constraint on LFL reaching objectives.

(A) The candidate goes correctly for the one piece of legislation that is 'flagged up' in the case and analyses it well — although presumably 'perspective changes' should read 'prospective changes'. Analysis is shown early in the answer.

(B) This is a very good point and demonstrates a sound understanding of how employees respond to changes in the labour market and therefore how the businesses they work for are also likely to be affected.

(C) The analysis continues to be well linked to LFL's objectives.

(D) This is another valid point, although to be analytical it needs to be more clearly linked to the business's objectives.

(E) Evaluation occurs here. Of course, it could be argued that effective promotion or a product that 'works' is actually the key factor in determining success, rather than adherence to copyright laws, but that is not the point. A judgement is made as to the most significant piece of legislation and, although the wording is a little clumsy, the point about resources is well made and is linked (albeit in passing) to LFL's objectives. **13/18 marks**

(3) Competition in the market brings both benefits and problems/challenges to LFL.

If another firm which has the resources to compete effectively enters the market then this may pose a severe threat. This threat would be to Tamara and Chris's objectives of growth and being able to retire at 50 years old.**A** This is because they may be forced to lower their prices so that they stay competitive. The cuts in price would certainly affect the profit margins unless they were able to reduce costs in production. This may not be easy.

However, even if a competitor enters the market it may not have the experience of the market and it will not have the marketing distribution contacts that LFL has and so this may give LFL the time to prepare a response and so ensure that the competitor does not get well established. In fact if Chris (who it says is 'the ideas man') has been doing his job properly he should have been preparing a strategy for this already. If LFL do not respond appropriately to any competition and just assume that they will automatically be able to keep all of their customers this is a mistake and although they may be able to 'hold on' at first, in the long run their business will suffer.[B] Objectives will not be met — at least not as easily.

Competition could be good for LFL as a business, as if new firms are entering the market this must be because that market is expanding and profits are rising or are expected to rise in the future. So the new firm could be a sign to LFL that the market is expanding and they could take advantage of this because they have skills and distribution contacts already. This means more sales, higher market share growth and so greater profit, if the opportunity is exploited properly through market research and then following this up with good marketing.

Also, competition is beneficial for LFL because there is now a greater need to provide the best product possible due to there being another substitute available. This then in turn makes LFL focus on the quality of the product and having a distinctive USP that sets them apart from the rest of the competition. Assuming that LFL can do this and stay ahead then they should benefit which could help them reach the objective of retiring early.[C]

Finally it may be the other way round. By this I mean another firm may leave LFL's market. This could be good for LFL as they should probably be able to take over some of its business. However if the other firm was not very successful perhaps there will not be very much extra profit.[D] Also if the competitor went bust because of things like not being paid on time by customers then LFL would have to ensure that if it took on those customers it adopted a different approach to payments.

It all depends on if a competitor enters or leaves and how powerful they are or were. It cannot be assumed that the new competitor or one leaving will necessarily be bad or necessarily be good.[E]

(A) It is good to get in a reference to Chris and Tamara's objectives rather than simply talking in general terms about 'the business being badly affected', which is how such answers are often phrased. It is a pity the point about not being able to reduce costs was not developed.

(B) This is a valid consequence of the competition and LFL's response is given (Level 3).

(C) It is pleasing to see that some positive effects of the emergence of competition are considered. The candidate goes further and points out that the benefits will only occur 'if the opportunity is exploited properly through market research and then following this up with good marketing' — Level 3 again for analysis.

(D) The wording is a bit clumsy but the point is certainly valid and just makes it into Level 3. As mentioned in the commentary on question 1, candidates should avoid phrases like 'went bust'.

(E) This is a rather 'throwaway' conclusion and is not worthy of Level 4. It is not a judgement and merely summarises the previous points. This is a pity as the preceding analysis was very sound. It would have been much better if the candidate had offered a balanced view and then offered a judgement on the extent to which LFL is likely to be affected. Significantly? Or hardly at all? **11/18 marks**

(4) The success of LFL will depend on many factors such as meeting customer needs and effective management of the business's resources, but it will also be significantly affected by the way the economic climate changes. The objectives of the business are to ensure profits continue to grow and to ensure that the founders of the business can retire early at 50. It is therefore fair to say that 'the success' of the business will depend on its ability to meet these objectives and the economic climate would have a significant impact on this.**A**

If the economy enters a period of boom then it is highly likely that the sales of the business will improve. The implication of the economic climate changing for the better is increased consumer spending in particular for luxury/non-essential items such as the products that LFL sell. This will mean that in the short term at least the business is likely to be more successful because they will enjoy greater volume of sales and therefore it is highly likely that profits will rise at a greater rate — meeting one of the objectives of Chris and Tamara. The implication therefore of an upturn in the economy would be greater spending and therefore greater success for LFL.

Therefore in an upturn it seems highly likely that the economic climate will affect the success of LFL by allowing more people to buy their e-products magazine and therefore the sales will rise. The implication of this will be that LFL is closer to its objectives and therefore is a more successful business.**B**

A change in the economic climate is going to lead to a rethink of the objectives of LFL if the change is for the worse — a recession where demand falls. This is because the objectives that they set are geared towards growing as a company. However, if there is a recession it is likely that a suitable new objective is going to be survival and then in the long run they can push for growth and for big profits whereas in the short run survival may be the best option as an objective.**C** So what counts as success for them may change if the state of the economy changes.

LFL will also be affected by government policy taken as a result of the state of the economy. It is possible to assume that the rise in GDP will increase spending which will lead to an increase in LFL's web sales as the amount of government spending will rise due to greater tax revenues as unemployment and benefit payment falls, and therefore the teachers may have bigger budgets which they are able to spend on extra teaching material such as this.**D**

However if the government is intending to reducing its budget deficit because the economy is not in a boom, it is clear that more sales may not be the case for LFL as there will be less government spending on education.**E** This will have great implications for the success of LFL which may struggle if even the universities and the teachers stop buying their material because of cuts to their budgets.

As well as increases/decreases in government spending the government may change taxes. These could be on an individual or on a company. If taxes are raised then spending will fall and again bring about the changes above — demand will fall. Cuts in tax to increase demand will increase demand for LFL. The same is true if the government alters interest rates.

The economy is an extremely important determinant of whether a particular decision should be taken. Chris needs to think very carefully about the Zambezee deal. It may offer 'certainty' but by being tied down to a 4-year contract it is clear that LFL is very dependent on the success of that company. Therefore during an economic downturn there is going to be less flexibility in how LFL can react to changes in the economy and government policy. The contract would mean LFL is legally bound to deal with Zambezee even if Chris and Tamara wanted the business to change direction in terms of sales because of the state of the economy. Resources would have to be devoted to the contract for legal reasons. In the worst case scenario Zambezee might collapse as a company and therefore the long-term survival of LFL could be compromised. Thus Chris must consider whether tying the future of the company to the fortunes of another when the state of the economy is uncertain is a good strategic decision.**F**

Thus in conclusion the economic climate has a very large impact on the success of LFL. The strategies/objectives and therefore the success of LFL will be affected to a great extent by a change in the economic climate. What is clear is that the effect that the change will have will depend on whether it is an upturn or a downturn. As has been said, the goods that LFL sell are non-essential items, after all the students could just read the textbook, or keep up to date via free news sites. The downturn/recession in the economy will lead to people withdrawing from the magazine subscriptions and therefore the success of LFL will be compromised as their profits will fall due to lower revenues unless they can find a way to cut costs.

The economy is one of the major factors influencing LFL's success. Whilst Chris and Tamara can guide the business in some ways, e.g. which products to sell, there is nothing they can do about the state of the economy or what the government does as a result. This of course does not mean that they cannot react when the economy changes. They always need a plan to deal with this.

(A) Defining 'success' by linking it to LFL's objectives is a good start to the answer.

(B) Sound analysis is offered in the second paragraph by linking the consequences of an upturn to the meeting of the firm's objectives.

(C) This is a valid analytical point, clearly recognising the issues surrounding the business's objectives and the state of the economy.

(D) Note that although the term 'economic cycle' is never used in the answer, this does not matter as the candidate obviously knows about it and the implications of it for the business in terms of sales and government policy — which is dealt with correctly here and in the next two paragraphs.

(E) It is pleasing to see that the candidate recognises that changes in the economic cycle bring changes to economic policy, although the obvious mention of the effect of interest rate changes on LFL's debt repayments (its gearing is high) is not made. The points that are made here are nevertheless very sound and are certainly analytical. As a minor point, the candidate really should know that it is the Bank of England and not the government which sets the rate of interest.

(F) This is an evaluative point — the economy can indeed be 'an extremely important determinant of whether a particular decision should be taken' and this is explained and justified well here. Note that such evaluation does not necessarily have to appear in the final few lines of an answer.

20/23 marks

✍ **The total mark for the paper is 70/90 — an A grade.**

Answer to case study: candidate B

(1) (a) Decision tree option

Expected value (EV) for the decision for software is £26,600.

EV for leasing is £6,800.

✍ The values are correct and so all **13 marks** are scored. This is a promising start to the paper. However, no working at all was shown and the mark could easily have been zero if a couple of mistakes had crept in — such as putting £2,660 for the first calculation or 'twisting' a figure on the second and writing (say) £8,600. Such mistakes are easily made in an examination and candidates should always show their working. **13/13 marks.**

(b) The first thing that Tamara and Chris need to consider is how likely the decision tree is to be accurate. Presumably all the figures in it are estimates that depend on their forecasts for the future. The probabilities are very difficult to estimate and a small change in these will change the results given by the decision tree. According to the decision tree it is suggested that LFL should invest in just the e-book software. There are many reasons for this, however they will have to take into account factors other than what the decision tree says.**A** The first thing that they will need to take into consideration will be the amount of money that they will need to borrow from the banks to make sure that there will be enough capital to make the venture work.

The fact that the e-book service only has a cost of £30,000 makes it initially a very attractive prospect. This is because it will mean that if the venture were to be unsuccessful then the financial burden, though large, would not have the same effect on the business as the hardware, which could leave the business with a very large amount of debt.**B** However they will need to take into consideration factors other than just the financial figures and calculations.

One thing that they will need to consider will be if they will be able to gain enough royalties from the venture, because there is the change that is coming into effect. This may mean for LFL that they will not gain as much revenue from the investment as would have been the case under the previous law.**C** This is more of a side concern that they will need to monitor with whatever course of action they take.

Another factor that they will need to consider is their current financial situation. The fact that they have a large amount of fixed assets means that if their investment were to fail, it would mean that they would be unable to repay the bank for the loan. However, the fact that they have nearly £30,000 of debt would mean that they would need to take this factor into consideration. If the venture were to fail, it would mean the amount of debt might be too great for them. They would be unlikely to be able to repay the money that they owed.**D**

A consideration that LFL will need to make will be the amount of money that they will make back over the immediate time after the launch of the product. The fact that the e-book has a smaller return rate should be taken into consideration. This will be of concern for Tamara because she would like to increase the profitability of the company so that she will be able to retire early. However, she will need to take into consideration how risky each of the investments is. The fact that the e-books are a fairly safe option will mean that the profitability of the venture may be smaller but it will be more of a guaranteed revenue generator.**E** The fact that the e-books and hardware represent a very large sum of money will mean that LFL may gain a greater amount of revenue and therefore profit, but they will have to borrow a large amount of money to make sure that the venture goes along without a hitch.

A final consideration that LFL will need to make before they make their decision will be the economic climate that is currently around. The fact that we are currently in a recession will mean that any type of lending will be restricted. So LFL will need to consider the effects that such a large amount of lending could have on their accounts.

Taking all these factors into account and considering the long term outlook for LFL, I would suggest that Tamara and Chris sell the software rather than consider leasing the hardware. The first option does not carry the same risks and this is a significant factor at a time when the economy is just emerging from recession and public sector spending is so tight. This will move them into a new market where they can use their existing marketing expertise.**F** They can always put the hardware option on hold for the long run when the economy picks up and schools have more money to spend.

(A) The answer starts off by considering the effectiveness of decision trees in determining what a business should do and considers the results given by this particular decision tree. The answer in this paragraph would achieve Level 2 because it shows understanding of the concept and the ability to explain the use of decision trees in practice. Although context is not needed to get Level 2 marks, the answer is in the context of LFL.

(B) and **(C)** The candidate goes on to look at the implications of the decision tree in more detail in the context of LFL. There is consideration of debts that the ventures will create and the likelihood that the business will be able to generate sufficient money to make the investment worthwhile. These paragraphs show the use of analysis by considering the impact of the investments on the financial situation of the business. They would gain Level 3 marks.

(D) The candidate then goes on to analyse the situation further by looking more carefully at the effect of borrowing on LFL.

(E) The candidate begins to evaluate the alternatives by considering and weighing up their relative risks for the business and the likelihood of success with each alternative. This starts to move the answer into the bottom of Level 4.

(F) Finally, the candidate comes to a weighted judgement that is supported by the analysis that has preceded it. This is further evidence of evaluation, which would move the answer higher into Level 4. The candidate could have considered using Ansoff's Matrix here. If possible, answers should contain both numerical and non-numerical analysis and evaluation. **14/18 marks**

(2) Legislation is any type of law that the government passes. These laws are often related to the way that a company treats its employees or the way it produces its product.**A**

One of the most obvious ways in which legislation could affect LFL would be if the government changed the national minimum wage. This would mean that LFL would have to pay a greater amount to its workers who are not on a salary. However this is likely to have a very limited effect on LFL because they are unlikely to have a large number of staff who would be working for minimum wage.**B** Even if the NMW was to increase it would be unlikely to be a large amount that would have any type of compound effect on the way that LFL operates.

Any changes to the payment of royalties could have a big impact on LFL and its revenue, particularly if it becomes the subject of legislation. This is an important factor for this business and it is important that Tamara and Chris start to make plans for the future. All businesses should have strategic plans in place for dealing with anticipated or catastrophic change in the external factors that might affect the business. Tamara and Chris need to find out all the details of the proposed changes and also how far the government is likely to be involved in legislating in this area. They need to be ready for the change when it happens so that they can make sure that the business's income is assured.**C** If they don't make these plans they are unlikely to be able to reach their objectives for the future.

All business is going to be the subject of different sorts of legislation, most of it with financial implications. For example the recent changes in employers' National Insurance contributions will have an effect on LFL. This will be like paying an extra 1% in taxes on their employees' salaries. Tamara and Chris need to ensure that they keep up-to-date with changes in the economy and government policy. They cannot afford to run the business in isolation from these external factors. Perhaps they should do regular SWOT analysis so that they are aware of any possible threats to the business from new legislation. Going through all these processes will help Tamara and Chris see how likely they are to achieve their objectives.**D** They may need to extend the date for retirement if the trading situation becomes difficult.

LFL is operating in a fast moving sector of the economy and it is likely that such a sector will be the subject of government interest from a variety of angles — data protection, child protection, censorship. Chris and Tamara need to be aware of these threats and they must plan for them, otherwise they might find themselves in a situation where revenue and profits are falling because of these external circumstances.**E** In these circumstances they may struggle to survive rather than be able to think about an early retirement and selling a successful business.

(A) The candidate achieves Level 1 at the start of the answer. The candidate shows that they understand what the term 'legislation' means.

(B) The answer moves on to Level 2, with explanations of legislation and examples of the sorts of law that might affect a business like LFL.

(C) The candidate then goes on to analyse the effects that new laws might have on LFL, giving examples that are in context and analysing their effects on the business.

(D) The candidate also analyses in a number of different ways the strategic implications for Chris and Tamara, in terms of planning for the future. The difference between anticipated and unanticipated change is explored.

(E) This is a further example of analysis at Level 3. However, the candidate fails to go on to evaluate the situation and the answer stays in Level 3. To achieve Level 4 the candidate needs to ensure that the changes raised are linked to Tamara and Chris's ability to achieve their objectives.

11/18 marks

(3) First of all LFL need to consider who their competition is. They need to look at their market and assess where they might face threats from new competition.

They need to consider other firms in their line of business, because there might be other publishing businesses that are facing the same decisions that they are.[A] These firms may be considering moving into the internet business because of difficulties in traditional publishing.

LFL should consider the options offered by Ansoff's Matrix. They could think about expanding their current market if there were opportunities available to them. The problem is that the market they are in seems to be very limited at the moment and the risk of staying in this area as their only market seems quite high.[B]

If LFL feel that their competitors are a threat, an alternative would be to transfer their current business to a new market like university students. They could make themselves the forerunners in this market and capture the business because they were the first providers. They would need to do careful market research first, but there could be good opportunities for them here, especially if more young people go to university because of the recession.[C] If they could get a foothold quickly there would be an opportunity to become market leaders ahead of the competition.

They could also think about looking at a new product which is what Tamara's alternative would offer. The risk here is that this is a completely new market and neither Tamara nor Chris knows whether there is the demand out there or that schools have the funds to move into leasing hardware. It may be that their competitors are already in this market and know more about it. If that is the case this would be a very risky option for LFL and one that would be unlike to achieve their strategic objectives.[C]

LFL need to think carefully about the future of their business and the way that the market is moving. They are in a fast moving market and it is difficult to anticipate the likely changes. The future of education and learning is difficult to predict. Added to that, public finance is also in a situation where there might be much less money available. If there is a cut in public spending, schools might find that they cannot afford new technology and that they have to rely on traditional teaching methods. In such a market the size and success of competitors will be crucial to LFL's success. If the competition is already established in the market and is a large or successful firm, LFL will be unlikely to be successful entering the market late in the day as a small scale provider.[C]

In these circumstances, the extent and quality of the competition in the market could be very significant. If one of the large internet firms like Microsoft enter the market, LFL are unlikely to be able to compete. These large firms have large amounts of capital at their disposal and they can afford to take risks. They have already diversified and they will not be so badly affected if part of their market fails. LFL, on the other hand, are fairly small scale and a failure in part of their market might be catastrophic for the future of the business.[D] It would certainly have an effect on their wish to retire at 50.

LFL needs to think carefully about who their competition is likely to be. If they think that they will be in a niche market and that they will be the first business in this market they might be well advised to take the plunge. If on the other hand they think that some major large scale businesses might want to move into this market, they should stop and think about the risks.[E] There is no way that a small business like LFL can have the capital, contacts and expertise to take on this sort of competition.

I would suggest that LFL do some market research into the market itself but that they also try to find out who else might be interested in moving into this market. The scale of the competition could be crucial to their likely success. On the one hand it could be far too risky to take on the competition; on the other hand they could find themselves dominating a profitable niche market. Only market research will tell them how much of a threat the competition is.[F]

(A) The first paragraph of the answer achieves Level 2 by explaining the fact that Tamara and Chris need to decide who constitutes their competition before they can start to decide to what extent they are affected by them.

(B) The answer wanders from the question by looking at the way that LFL should respond to competition. It is important to keep the question in your mind at all times. Normally, the correct use of Ansoff's Matrix would earn Level 3 marks. Although the discussion is correct, the candidate does not achieve Level 3 because the answer is not relevant to the question.

(C) The candidate begins to analyse the situation and earns Level 3 marks for a number of points. There is consideration of the size, success and nature of the competition and the state of the market that LFL are considering moving into.

(D) The analysis is improved at this point where the candidate compares and considers the likely competitors with LFL and its chances of success. The candidate also considers the impact of the decision on Tamara and Chris's likelihood of achieving their objective.

(E) The comments here would take the answer to the top of Level 3. There is consideration of the nature of the market, and the comments about the extent to which it is a niche market offer good analysis.

(F) Finally the answer comes to a weighted judgement about the extent to which LFL might be affected by the competition and how Tamara and Chris should approach this situation. Of course, from the information given, it is impossible to say how much impact competition will have. However, it is possible to comment on the various possibilities, as the candidate has done. He or she could have achieved a higher Level 4 by considering factors such as the effect of competition on market share, profitability or pricing policy. **14/18 marks**

(4) The market for LFL's products will be very much affected by changes in the economy. As it says in the case study, at a time of recession when there are not as many jobs available, more school leavers are likely to go on to higher education.**A** At the same time, in these situations, the government might struggle to put as much money into the education sector.

LFL's market will be very much affected by the amount of public spending. The spending on LFL's services will come from a limited sector of the economy. Their services are bought at present by students and schools. The services that they offer are by no means essential and they are likely to have high income elasticity of demand. This means that if personal income is tight, students may decide not to buy their publications. This could create problems for LFL in retaining their income levels.**B** Added to this, schools, universities and local authorities may also feel that they cannot afford to buy the publications and services that they offer. If the government finds that finance is tight because of the state of the economy, the sort of services offered by LFL could easily be sacrificed.

LFL will be very much affected by any changes in economic activity. Although their core business might be secure, they are likely to suffer if the economy goes into recession and income levels in the economy decline. LFL needs to make strategic plans for this sort of situation. They need to ensure that they can maintain their revenue whilst looking for new markets that might be less affected by recession.**C**

It is true that more students are likely to go to further education if jobs are scarce, but these students might not have much money at their disposal. In these circumstances the 4-year contract with Zambezee might be the best solution. This gives them some security for the future. In addition, e-books might be a better idea for students than the cost of buying actual books. This will give LFL the security of a contract together with the expertise and marketing abilities of an established business.**C**

Tamara and Chris's plans to retire before they are 50 might need to be put on hold if the economy goes into recession. This is not the best time to be thinking of making large amounts of money. What they need instead is some sort of security and certainty for the short to medium term so that in the long term, when the economy picks up, they can make use of their new markets to improve their revenue. A time when the economy is uncertain and the government is cutting back on public sector spending is not a good time to move into a new venture.**D** Maybe Chris and Tamara should get this new leasing system ready for an upturn in economic activity.

I would suggest that LFL should be careful of how they move if there is an economic downturn. Their strategy should be to make the most of the strengths of the business and the contacts they have whilst making strategic plans for the long term so that they are ready to move into new markets when the economy picks up.**E** Good strategic planning in the short term will help them to survive through the downturn and plan for the future so that they are ready, in the long term, for when the economy picks up.

(A) The answer begins by explaining how a change in the economic climate would affect LFL. In this case the candidate is using a decline in economic activity. It is only necessary to explain what happens in one direction. Do not waste time by going on to explain the opposite situation of the economy picking up.

(B) The candidate then goes on to analyse the effects of a downturn on LFL's business. The whole of the paragraph is in context and uses good analysis, achieving Level 3 marks. In particular, the correct use of elasticity to explain the likely effects will usually take an answer to Level 3.

(C) The candidate goes on to analyse the situation in more detail, looking at the need for a strategic plan to weather the economic downturn, and making a comparison between the likely merits of the two alternatives that LFL is considering.

(D) The answer moves into evaluation by considering the short- and long-term decisions that Tamara and Chris need to make. The answer weighs up the alternatives and looks at how these alternatives could help them meet their objectives. It achieves Level 4 in this paragraph. It would, however, have been better to discuss the situation in terms of profitability and increased revenue, rather than 'making more money'.

(E) Finally the candidate comes to a weighted conclusion about how Tamara and Chris should act. It is not necessary to offer a conclusion unless the question specifically asks for one. If it does, you must give a conclusion that you have justified. In this case the candidate's conclusion helps move the answer further up into Level 4 by considering the effects in a time-based framework of the short and long term. Throughout this question it is important that all points are linked to the success of LFL. **19/23 marks**

The paper achieves 71/90, which is a grade A.

■ ■ ■

Appendix

Detailed mark scheme

Question (1)

(a) ARR and payback

For e-book software alone, payback occurs (i.e. the initial investment is recouped) after 2 years 4 months.

The ARR is 26.7%.

Inflows 62 K. Initial cost 30 K. Net inflow = 32 K

32 K/4 years = 8 K

8/30 = 26.7%

For software and hardware leasing, payback occurs (i.e. the initial investment is recouped) after 2 years 3 months.

The ARR is 37.5%.

Inflows 550 K. Initial cost 220 K. Net inflow = 330 K

330/4 years = 82.5 K

82.5/220 = 37.5%

Level 3: The answer contains analysis of the ARR/payback technique(s) to determine the payback/ARR value(s). [13–9 marks]

Maximum marks can only be achieved by 4 correct answers.

4 correct answers with no working score 13 marks.

Only 1 correct answer with an attempt at the other calculations scores 12.

If only ARR is attempted, award 9–11.

If only payback is attempted, award 9–11.

Level 2: Applies understanding of the ARR/payback technique(s) in attempting to determine ARR/payback value(s). [8–4 marks]

Up to 2 marks for each ARR and payback calculation attempted but with an incorrect answer. If only one technique is attempted, maximum mark is 4.

Level 1: Demonstrates some knowledge of the ARR/payback technique. [3–1 marks]

Formula(s) given/techniques(s) defined.

Question (1)

(a) Decision tree

Level 3: The answer contains analysis of the decision tree technique to determine the expected value(s). [13–9 marks]

Maximum marks can only be achieved by both correct answers.

Both correct answers with no working score 13 marks.

One correct calculation with an attempt at the other calculation scores 12.

OFR applies.

EV of selling software is £26,600.

$62K \times 0.8 = 49.6K$

$35K \times 0.2 = 7K$

$EV = 56.6K - 30K = 26.6K$

EV of leasing software is £6,800

$146.5K \times 0.2 = 29.3K$

$350K \times 0.5 = 175K$

$75K \times 0.3 = 22.5K$

$EV = 226.8K - 220K = 6.8K$

If only selling software considered, award 9–11.

If only leasing considered, award 9–11.

Level 2: Applies understanding of the decision tree technique in attempting to determine expected value(s). [8–4 marks]

2 marks for each 'payoff' $\times$ probability calculation attempted up to a maximum of 8. OFR

If only one branch is attempted, maximum 4.

Level 1: Demonstrates some knowledge of the decision tree technique. [3–1 marks]

Techniques(s) defined.

Statement(s) made about EV, chance events, etc. with no attempt to apply to LFL.

Question (1)

(b) How reliable are the probabilities and payoff figures?

EMVs are not guaranteed amounts.

Techniques such as this can try to estimate the effects of different causes of action but cannot make the decision for Tamara and Chris. What other considerations are there?

Consideration of ARR and payback data.

For software alone these figures are 26.7% and 2 years 4 months.

For software leasing these figures are 37.5% and 2 years 3 months.

Other issues. Likelihood of raising the finance for the software leasing? Implications of balance sheet? The business is highly geared.

Tamara and Chris's attitude to risk.

Opportunity costs of their time launching each?

How does each new proposed product fit existing portfolio?

Which is most likely to achieve LFL's objectives?

Level 4: Discussion is balanced in evaluating recommendation.   [18–12 marks]

Level 3: Analyses case material in support of recommendation.   [11–8 marks]

Level 2: Recommendation is supported by descriptive use of the material.   [7–4 marks]

Level 1: Offers a view without support.   [3–1 marks]

■ ■ ■

Question (2)

Objectives are:

For both to retire before they are 50.

For profits to continue to grow ... at an even faster rate.

The copyright laws are mentioned in the case. The issues here are that it is not as good for the author — 'publishing software and internet resources are less easy to control and their royalties less easy to attribute' — but it will be easier for the publisher. This may help LFL to reach their objective quicker. Of course, any authors wanting to 'sign up' with LFL will want to ensure that they get their royalties and Chris and Tamara will have to devote time to this. If authors do not get 'the right amount' of royalties, they will not be happy. Opportunity cost to this time will take them from other activities that may impact on growth of profits.

Would employing someone else to check who needs paying/has been paid be sensible? Cost of this? Effect on profits?

Answers do not have to focus on this and any reasonable change to a piece of legislation is acceptable e.g. health and safety — may be necessary to do an audit. Opportunity cost of time. Costs of formulating a new policy. Training issues. Implications of non-compliance.

Minimum wage changes.

Level 4: Discussion is balanced in evaluating recommendation.   [18–12 marks]

Level 3: Analyses case material in support of recommendation.   [11–8 marks]

Level 2: Recommendation is supported by descriptive use of the material.   [7–4 marks]

Level 1: Offers a view without support.   [3–1 marks]

■■■

Question (3)

Who are the competitors? Other online publications? Or 'ordinary' existing booksellers?

Short- versus long-term effects.

To what extent does **LFL** have a **USP** (and is therefore difficult to compete against)?

How contestable is their market? Easy to enter? Start-up costs high/low? New entrants may not have the contacts that **LPL** has and/or only a small amount of finance to try to penetrate the market. On the other hand, a business which is (say) a subsidiary of a large existing company may have access to finance to compete.

New competition may not affect **LPL** if they have adopted a strategic plan to cope with this eventuality, e.g. promotional campaign to 'hang on' to existing customers.

Effects on LFL if a competitor leaves the market?

Level 4: Discussion is balanced in evaluating the extent of the effect(s) of competition on LFL.   [18–12 marks]

Level 3: Analyses case material in support of consideration of the effect(s) of competition on LFL.   [11–8 marks]

Level 2: Descriptive use of the material when considering the effect(s) of competition on LFL.   [7–4 marks]

Level 1: Offers knowledge of competitors/competitors' possible actions.   [3–1 marks]

■■■

Question (4)

State of economy on economic cycle: boom/recession/recovery?

Fiscal/monetary policy changes. Likely response of government and/or Bank of England to position on cycle.

Effect of changes in interest rates on LFL? Consideration of effects on loans the business has/may take out. Balance sheet shows high gearing. Higher interest payments mean more resources devoted to repaying loan(s).

Consideration of how long any changes in the economy/economic policy are likely to last and therefore subsequent effect on consumer and LPL behaviour.

How income elastic are the business's products?

Would the exchange rate have any effect? Might have if LPL decide to sell abroad in future.

Level 4: Discussion is balanced in evaluating how the economy might affect the success of LFL. [23–17 marks]

Level 3: Analyses case material when considering how the economy might affect the success of LFL. [16–11 marks]

Level 2: Descriptive use of the material when considering how the economy might affect the success of LFL. [10–5 marks]

Level 1: Offers knowledge of economy/economic factors/economic policy. [4–1 marks]